NOT NORMAL

2010-2014

Dena Selby, MD

Compiled and Edited by Dena Selby, M.D.

ISBN-10: 1502834235
ISBN-13: 978-1502834232

DEDICATION

To Tom, my husband; and Kandra and Jessica, our daughters. The three of you provide me with strength, love, and inspiration.

To family, friends, and pets everywhere, the elixir of a good life.

INTRODUCTION

Haines is a well kept secret of Alaska. This rural town of 2,500 people is often called "The Adventure Capitol of the World." Haines has all the amenities of a small town, located in a spectacular scenic setting. The town offers many activities to provide unique memories for visitors from air, land and sea.

Living the Alaskan rural life is often difficult for people from Outside to comprehend. A sampling of comments from visitors to Haines include the following:

-What elevation are we at? (sea level; your cruise ship docked at the pier)

-Do you take American money? (we are the 49th state of the U.S.A. as of January 3, 1959)

-What a pretty lake you have here! (how can it be a lake if your ship arrived here via the Lynn Canal)

-I know you don't have state tax, so what is this "donkey" tax we must pay on our purchases? (Haines is a "Borough" and has in-town borough tax)

-Does the courtesy shuttle stop at a Walmart? (uh, do you realize you are in a small, RURAL town in Alaska)

-Summertime question: What time do the bears come out? (whenever they feel like it)

Residents of Haines have their own list of interesting and sometimes entertaining occurrences. These are best found in the "Police Blotter" published on the Haines Borough Police Department Facebook page or in the weekly newspaper.

This book includes a sampling of the Police Blotter inclusive of the years 2010 through 2014. The reading material is divided into the seasons, as well as special topics that occur seasonally in Haines, so the reader can experience living five full years in Haines. Sometimes there is overlap between "The Seasons" and different human and animal activity. This helps the reader appreciate what activities are happening at different times of the year.

Because of deliberate concise editing, the grammatical syntax in the Blotter often creates an amusing entry. This should not be interpreted as irrational behavior. My intention is to highlight the excellent police and civilian work accomplished every day in our small town.

The reader might notice pronouns varying from singular to plural within the same sentence. This allows the entries to remain gender neutral. When noted, the time of the report is indicated with the 24-hour clock.

The following chapters include excerpts from the Police Blotter that should not remain in obscurity, but be presented to the world for absolutely no reason that I can think of.

Respectively submitted,

Dena Selby, M.D.

p.s. any italics in the police blotter entries are mine.

1

HAINES, ALASKA

CONTENTS

abbreviations used:

AST: *Alaska State Troopers*
DOT: *Department of Transportation*
F&G: *Field & Game*
HARK: *Haines Animal Rescue Kennel*
HBPD: *Haines Borough Police Department*
KHNS: *The local radio station of Haines/Skagway*
SEARHC: *SouthEast Alaska Regional Health Consortium*

ACKNOWLEDGMENTS

Thank you to the many police who served Haines during this time, and the dispatchers who triage the calls and document the incidents to be later transformed into the concise "Police Blotter" entries that are shared with the public. A portion of the proceeds of this book will be donated to a charity of their choice. Thank you also to the people of Haines, who, along with the spectacular scenery, make the Borough of Haines the place where my soul lives all year round.

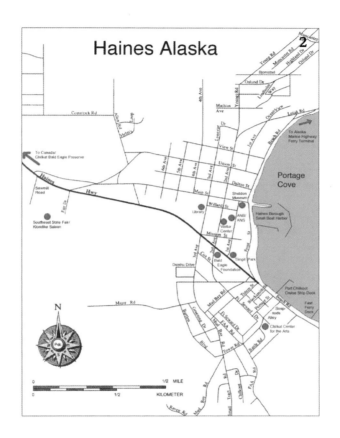

MAP OF HAINES TOWNSITE

9

1) RURAL LIFE

Tuesday, January 5, 2010	A person was shot in the foot when their gun accidentally discharged. Officer responded.
Tuesday, January 5, 2010	Caller reported a person drinking beer in a parked vehicle. Officer advised. Caller called back to apologize; it was not beer but an organic pop.
Sunday, January 10, 2010	Caller reported they set off the fire alarm while cooking at Haines Assisted Living, no fire emergency.
Monday, January 11, 2010	Caller reported a boat broke loose and drifted up onto the beach at Letnikof Cove. Harbormaster and AST advised.
Wednesday, January 13, 2010	Caller reported they parked at the bottom of their street because they couldn't make it up and to let them know if it was in the way of the snow removal and they would move it. Officer and Public Works advised.
Thursday, February 18, 2010	Multiple callers reported an airplane circling over Haines. Officer advised. They were waiting for the fog to lift in Juneau.
Tuesday, March 9, 2010	Caller reported two people used the school showers and did not pay the $2.00 per person fee. Officer advised.
Tuesday, March 30, 2010	An agency requested an officer check the airport to make sure it was clear for a helicopter landing. Officer responded.
Sunday, May 16, 2010	Caller requested an officer go to their house and speak with their 16-year-old son who was giving them problems.
Monday, May 17, 2010	Caller reported a youth threw a .22 bullet into a barbecue and was worried for the children's safety. Officer advised.

Saturday, May 29, 2010	Caller requested information on taxi service for a truck driver stranded at 3 Mile Haines Highway. The caller was told there is no taxi service in town.
Thursday, October 14, 2010	A downtown resident reported a rifle missing. The firearm was later discovered to have been taken by a friend, who was cleaning it.
Saturday, January 22, 2011	Person reported the American Flag had blown off the flagpole at the Bank. Bank notified.
Saturday, April 9, 2011	Caller reported a reckless driver, an officer responded and citations made (*Editor's note: the story circulated is - driver drove up onto a Main Street sidewalk and hit a sign and a fire hydrant. The caller later reported the sign knocked over in the street was causing a hazard*).
Sunday, April 24, 2011	A person reported that some fishermen were seen with 24 Dolly Varden next to them on the Chilkat River (*above the limit of 10 per day*). AST was advised.
Sunday, May 8, 2011	Police confiscated a gun for safe keeping out of an unsecured vehicle that was unattended in the school parking lot.
Thursday, May 12, 2011	A patrolling officer spotted an illegal burn. Officer contacted the individual and cited them for burning after 8 p.m.
Saturday, May 28, 2011	Person reported 2 or 3 children that are at the school playground and appear to have lost their parents. Officer responded and the children had been picked up by their parents.
Friday, June 10, 2011	Caller reported his vehicle had been stolen. Border and ferry officials were advised. Caller reported back shortly after to advise that a friend had borrowed the car when their vehicle had broken down and everything is okay now.

Monday, June 27, 2011	Park Ranger reported a vehicle has been parked in the same spot for a couple days and would like the owners contacted to make sure everything is okay. Owner stated last thing he knew about the car it was at the ferry terminal but a friend might have used it.
Friday, July 15, 2011	Caller reported their vehicle was stolen, it was discovered the vehicle was borrowed accidentally.
Friday, July 22, 2011	U.S. Coast Guard relayed a message from a boater that they saw a large brush fire out Lutak Road. Officer made contact with the owner of the land who stated they are burning 160 acres worth of brush and the landowner has a current burn permit.
Friday, September 16, 2011	Officers responded to provide backup for state troopers after a man turned in a sub-legal moose to Fish and Game and became upset.
Tuesday, September 20, 2011	Caller requested an officer go to the Port Chilkoot Dock and turn on the lights as they were unable to contact the harbormaster and are en route to Haines.
Wednesday, September 21, 2011	Caller requesting the lights be turned on at the Port Chilkoot Dock as they do not know where the switch is. Officer responded.
Tuesday, January 31, 2012	A caller reported he was advised by relatives of two earthquakes near Oceanside. Officer responded and advised there is no road hazard at this time but there is a new crack.
Friday, April 6, 2012	An officer assisted troopers by responding to caller at 10 Mile Lutak Road who reported hearing gunshots. The officer located a group of people who said they were shooting off bottle rockets and a BB gun.

Saturday, April 14, 2012	A caller reported the theft of her bicycle; the caller later reported that the bicycle had been returned.
Friday, July 27, 2012	A walk-in reported firewood bundles he had for sale on his property, valued at $30.00, was taken and not paid for. An officer located the firewood taker, who returned and paid for it.
Saturday, August 18, 2012	A boat was reported by authorities as sunk while tied up at the Letnikof Cove Harbor.
Saturday, November 24, 2012	A box of household items was found at .5 Mile Small Tracts Road. Messages were left on the community website and KHNS.
Friday, December 7, 2012	A local business owner reported a vehicle parked an inordinately long time in front of another business (*Editor's note: there is a one-hour parking restriction downtown*). Officers contacted the owner, who moved the vehicle.
Friday, December 21, 2012	Caller reported a neighbor's roof tin was being blown off by the wind and that he was going to attempt to have it replaced as she is out of town.
Monday, June 10, 2013	1320: An assembly member requested officer presence at the assembly chambers due to an unruly assembly audience. An officer responded.
Friday, August 30, 2013	Caller reported a man yelling and screaming in the Front Street area (the man was apparently bellowing, "I'm walking down the street").
Wednesday, September 18, 2013	Caller reported an unsecured rifle outside the public library. A man had his rifle in his backpack and had left it near the library's front doors. Police investigated and did not find a rifle or the male described by the caller.

Wednesday, September 18, 2013	1952: A caller reported seeing what appeared to be her own property (a chair) at another neighbor's garage sale.
Sunday, May 11, 2014	A person on the Battery Point Trail asked for help from the Haines Animal Rescue Kennel pulling porcupine quills from a dog. HARK was advised.
Friday, June 13, 2014	A person reported seeing a confused man carrying a rifle near Main Street. Police responded but were unable to locate the man.

Friday, July 25, 2014	0255: An earthquake measuring approximately Magnitude 6 just occurred. Three calls were received about the quake, but no damage or injuries were reported. Tsunami Center advised there was no Tsunami danger.
Monday, July 28, 2014	A citizen reported observing an officer wave to the driver of a vehicle that had not signaled while making a turn on 2nd Avenue and Main Street. The citizen discussed the issue with the chief of police. Officer saw the vehicle stop at the 4 way, yield to pedestrians and a family on bikes, and then make a safe right hand turn - had not noticed the lack of turn signal - and our officers always try to wave back at those who wave at us.
Monday, August 4, 2014	A resident reported a party at a nearby baseball field. Officers responded and found children playing baseball.
Monday, August 4, 2014	0724: Caller requested information as to why the border was closed was advised that those regulations were set by U.S. Customs (*Editor's note: the Dalton Cache border station is closed from 11:00 pm to 7:00 am 365 days a year*).
Monday, September 22, 2014	0822: A caller on Piedad Road reported hearing the sound of two gun shots being fired. A HBPD officer was advised. Duck season open with hunting down by the river.
Saturday, December 13, 2014	1814: A pilot called in to report that the airport lights were on and had been on for several days. DOT was contacted and they advised that they are waiting for a part to come in, in order to fix the lights. The caller was updated.

Sunday, December 14, 2014	0726: A caller in the Fort Seward area reported seeing a vehicle with the door open and the dome light on. He requested a HBPD officer respond to investigate. HBPD officer made contact with the owner of the vehicle and determined that the seatbelt had stuck in the door blocking it from closing. Nothing was missing from the vehicle.

Saturday, August 9, 2014	1830: A caller reported vehicles parked in the road on Mud Bay Road restricting traffic to one lane, believed to be related to a wedding in the area.	
	 4	 5

2) SPRING

Tuesday, May 4, 2010	An Anchorage caller reported an overdue traveler that was last heard from in Haines. Canadian Border Patrol advised.
Thursday, May 6, 2010	An officer had to prevent an altercation at a local bar when a man mistakenly thought another person at the bar had hit his son earlier in the day with their vehicle (his son had been on a bicycle).
Saturday, May 29, 2010	An officer ordered campfires at Port Chilkoot Beach to be doused because of the burn ban and also ordered people swimming in the nude to get dressed.

Sunday, March 13, 2011	Multiple callers reporting no water, and that there was a leak in between the American Bald Eagle Foundation and the Post Office. Water and Sewer advised.
Wednesday, March 30, 2011	Caller reported a fire hydrant at Fish and Game had a four-foot sink hole around it. Public works was advised.
Friday, April 1, 2011	Caller reported rocks in the incoming lane on Lutak Road. An officer responded and removed the rocks.
Tuesday, April 5, 2011	Caller reported a lot of smoke on Mud Bay Road and thought someone was burning. An officer responded and found several smoking chimneys but no one burning.
Wednesday, April 6, 2011	Caller reported a neighbor took items from their yard without permission. An officer was advised. It was later discovered the neighbor had used a rake and a shovel to get rocks off the road.
Friday, April 29, 2011	Multiple callers reported a large boulder in the road just past the ferry terminal. DOT advised.
Wednesday, May 4, 2011	A local business reported they received a bad check a year ago and have been working with the person about paying and would like now to press charges as they have not yet paid. Officer advised and case initiated.
Saturday, May 7, 2011	Caller reported a water leak at their house right next to the water meter. Water and Sewer crew advised.
Saturday, May 7, 2011	Caller reported possible shots being fired out on the water. Troopers and officer responded and made contact with the individuals when they came back to the harbor. They had been shooting from a boat.

Monday, May 9, 2011	Caller reported a purse had been stolen out of their vehicle at a local business. Officer responded and the missing purse was located in the business.
Friday, May 13, 2011	Person reporting a rock slide at 8.5 mile Haines Highway and that the northbound lane was blocked. DOT responded.
Saturday, May 14, 2011	The landfill stated someone did not come back and pay their fee. Officer responded and made contact with the individual that left and he stated that he would be in on Monday to pay the fee.
Sunday, May 15, 2011	Person reported seeing a man lying in a boat floating down the river and was concerned they might have been hurt or passed out. AST responded and located the man, who reported he was sleeping in his boat a few minutes prior to the trooper's arrival.
Monday, June 6, 2011	Caller reported three vehicles parked in the no parking zone at the Port Chilkoot Dock. The caller stated that someone had removed the 'no parking' signs also. An officer responded and issued warnings.
Saturday, April 7, 2012	Caller reported two planes flying low over the Highway at 33 Mile. AST advised and forwarded information to the Federal Aviation Administration.

Tuesday, April 10, 2012	A kiteboarder was in distress near Pyramid Island but was aided to shore in a canoe prior to the ambulance arrival.
Thursday, April 12, 2012	A 911 call was determined to be a pocket dial from a cell phone. The caller was warned for recurring calls from his malfunctioned cell phone, as accidental calls could impede an actual emergency.
Friday, April 13, 2012	A caller complained about kids on skateboards at the intersection of 2nd Avenue and Main Street; an officer responded and warned the kids. Skateboarders also were reported at that intersection on April 11 (*Editor's note: skateboarders are not allowed on the roadway or on sidewalks in the downtown business area*).
Tuesday, April 17, 2012	The interim harbormaster reported finding an inoperable firearm in the harbor dumpster, a second caller claimed that the firearm was his.

Saturday, April 21, 2012	A caller reported children throwing fire crackers at an apartment complex; an officer responded and found that the children were playing with "snap caps".
Sunday, April 22, 2012	Caller reported an airplane landing on Haines Highway at 33 Mile. AST advised. The landing was legal, according to Federal Aviation Administration regulations.
Saturday, April 28, 2012	An officer observed improper disposal of materials at a former place of business and served the owner with notice of inappropriate handling of bear attractant materials.
Wednesday, May 9, 2012	Caller complained of someone shooting a gun at 7 Mile Haines Highway but was advised this was not illegal.
Thursday, May 10, 2012	Public works reported a vehicle that had been abandoned for over a year. The owner of the vehicle was notified to move it.
Friday, May 11, 2012	Caller reported finding a discarded vehicle registration tag. Dispatch advised the caller that the tags had been discarded by the registered owner.

Saturday, May 12, 2012	Caller reported that participants in the bike/walk event were creating a hazardous situation for drivers at 17 to 19 Mile Haines Highway. AST advised.
Tuesday, May 15, 2012	A chimney fire was reported on Beach Road. Fire department personnel were dispatched. Prior to their arrival, the owner was able to put out the fire.
Thursday, May 17, 2012	Caller reported a paraglider he had observed from binoculars may be in distress. It was determined that the subject was fine and no accident had occurred.
Thursday, May 17, 2012	A caller reported two people shooting guns in the city limits. Officer made contact and the subjects agreed to discontinue after learning they were in the townsite and in violation.
Friday, May 18, 2012	An officer assisted the Civil Air Patrol in locating an emergency locator beacon that was going off. The device was located at the old sawmill in a junked car.
Saturday, June 2, 2012	A walk-in reported that his tent had been lost off his motorcycle between Chilkat State Park and town.
Sunday, June 3, 2012	A person walked into the police station seeking a ride to 25 Mile. Dispatch called a taxi (*Editor's note: Haines had a taxi service at this time; sometimes there is no taxi business here*).
Tuesday, June 26, 2012	A local hotel requested an officer to assist a guest who was intoxicated who did not know which room they were staying in.
Friday, June 29, 2012	Dispatch received three accidental 911 "pocket" dials.

Saturday, July 28, 2012	Intoxicated persons were reportedly swimming in the nude at the Port Chilkoot Dock beach. Police investigated and advised the individuals of Haines decency laws and drinking in public. Alcohol was disposed of.
Tuesday, October 9, 2012	A caller reported that there appeared to be smoke coming from the direction of Taiyasanka Harbor. Fire personnel investigated and found it to be steam coming off of the far side.
Thursday, April 18, 2013	A Mosquito Lake resident reported fireworks going off for an hour after 1:00 a.m. and reported this as an ongoing disturbance.
Saturday, April 20, 2013	A beeping alarm was reported coming from a vacant house on 3rd Avenue. The alarm was determined to be a malfunctioning smoke detector.
Sunday, April 21, 2013	Caller reported a burn barrel fire had gotten out of hand. Fire personnel responded, but the fire had already been contained.
Monday, April 22, 2013	Caller reported a possible safety hazard for a residence due to an "unusual situation regarding insects."
Monday, April 22, 2013	A person anonymously reported a driver with a court order for IID (Ignition Interlock Device) was driving without one.
Monday, April 22, 2013	Multiple complaints were received regarding a helicopter landing in a residential neighborhood and multiple gunshots being fired in the Mosquito Lake area.
Wednesday, April 23, 2013	Caller reported seeing a felon in possession of a firearm. An officer confirmed the report and advised the appropriate federal agency.

Tuesday, May 7, 2013	Caller reported a vehicle accident at 17 Mile Haines Highway. A vehicle struck a large piece of wood that had rolled out of the back of an in-bound vehicle, with estimated damage at $3,000.00.
Saturday, May 18, 2013	Caller reported a driver was driving recklessly, speeding down Allen Road with his head out the window. Police searched the area, but were unable to locate the vehicle.
Friday, May 24, 2013	1153: Caller reported someone had entered her residence and stole a can of paint and left trash on the kitchen floor.
Monday, May 27, 2013	2016: Caller reported an unauthorized burn above 4th Avenue. Police responded and the fire was extinguished.
Tuesday, May 28, 2013	A man from out of town requested help getting a background check performed, as Canadian authorities had stopped him at the border. The caller was advised of the appropriate office number to contact.
Friday, June 14, 2013	Dispatch received a 911 call from a Barnett Drive resident who said her house was beginning to flood. Investigation revealed the toilet was overflowing.. The caller requested dispatch to call a friend that would be able to help her. An officer and the caller's friend responded.
Sunday, March 9, 2014 --this is after 15" snowfall	0651: A caller reported being trapped in the cabin of his boat at the Small Boat Harbor due to the amount of snow fall. Harbormaster was advised and assisted.
Sunday, November 23, 2014	No entries - not even a pocket dial.

9

Wednesday, May 15: A rock slide at Mile 9 Haines Highway. Photograph taken after DOT cleared some large boulders from the roadway.

Haines Police
April 24

10

With the arrival of warmer weather, we are starting to hear a few reports of bears waking up and wandering around, so it seems like a good time to remind everyone to please keep your homes free from things that are likely to attract bears. Each year, the police department responds to many calls in Haines where bears have come onto someone's property and become a nuisance. More often than not, we have discovered that the bear had been attracted to the location because of the presence of something that the bear identified as a potential food source. In response to this pattern, the Borough passed ordinance HBC 8.20. This law requires
all organic waste material to be kept in a completely enclosed structure or container, except on the morning of garbage pickup, when the material can be placed outside in a garbage can with a tight fitting cover. Each person who owns and/or is in control of property that creates, maintains, or permits a bear attraction nuisance on the property may be charged with an infraction and subject to a fine of up to $300.00

Please minimize bear encounters in town by properly storing your garbage. If you see a bear within the townsite, please notify the Haines Borough Police Department, and we will take action to dissuade the bear from remaining within town. Once a bear gets used to finding garbage at a certain location, he is much more likely to return there and it is much more difficult for the police to convince the bear to permanently leave the area. We would much rather ask for the public's cooperation than write tickets, but we will be enforcing this ordinance when we see violations. If you have any questions about this ordinance, please feel free to contact the Haines Borough Police Department

4) SUMMER

11

12

It's tourist - and bear - season in Haines

Posted: Thursday, May 10, 2012 12:20 pm | Updated 1:52 pm, Wed Jan 16, 2013

By Fairbanks Daily News-Miner

Here's a funny item that appeared in the Haines police blotter on Wednesday. For those who don't know, Haines is a small town in Southeast Alaska that is located on the Haines Highway about 40 miles from the U.S./Canada border. It's only fitting that the call came on the day the first cruise ship of the season docked in Haines.

A tourist advised there were bears running loose near the Chilkoot River Bridge.
Caller: Hi, I am visiting from (out of state) and we drove out towards Chilkoot and when we went over the bridge...I just wanted to report that there were some bears there...running around loose.
Dispatch: Welcome to Haines.
Caller: Oh, is that normal?
Dispatch: That's where they live...Now, if they are threatening anybody or if you don't feel safe, please feel free to call back. Otherwise, just enjoy the wildlife.

Friday, June 4, 2010	Caller reported smoke across the channel from Battery Point. Firemen were advised and determined it was a rain cloud.
Friday, June 11, 2010	Troopers were advised after caller reported a camera crew trespassed into the Thunderbird House in Klukwan without permission.
Sunday, June 13, 2010	A person reported a possible "wanted" person was back in town. Troopers were advised and said the person was not wanted.
Wednesday, June 16, 2010	Caller used a gas station emergency phone to get assistance from a gas attendant but called 911 instead.
Thursday, June 17, 2010	Firemen reported a person on Oslund Drive having an unauthorized burn. The person was told about the requirement for a burn permit and notifying police of intended burns.
Saturday, June 19, 2010	Caller reported a young child locked inside the Port Chilkoot dock restrooms. The child unlocked the door before an officer arrived.
Tuesday, June 22, 2010	A fireman responded when caller reported a foul smell coming from the burn barrel of a neighbor near 1 Mile Haines Highway. The fireman advised a person not to burn plastic and styrofoam.
Tuesday, June 22, 2010	Caller reported a neighbor burning amid trees.
Friday, June 25, 2010	Caller reported a person regularly drove on the grass near their Fort Seward property. An officer responding found the area was a borough right-of-way.

Sunday, June 27, 2010	Caller on 4th Avenue reported a person hit them in the head with their purse.
Monday, June 28, 2010	A person reported they were dropped off at a 4th Avenue home while a person was going out drinking and driving. The caller wanted police to know they weren't drinking.
Tuesday, August 10, 2010	Caller reported a film crew standing on their vehicle to film inside the State Trooper's Office. Troopers were advised.
Saturday, August 14, 2010	The wildlife trooper was advised of a call about possibly illegal subsistence fishing at the mouth of Chilkoot River.
Saturday, August 14, 2010	A bicyclist reported a pedestrian had yelled obscene comments at them more than three times.
Saturday, August 14, 2010	Police received multiple calls about an orange light on the side of Santa Claus Mountain. An officer responding determined it was a campfire.
Sunday, August 15, 2010	A Deishu Drive caller reported a bad smell coming from a neighbor's place. An officer found a cooler full of rotten fish and attempted to contact the owner.
Monday, August 16, 2010	Caller reported a canoe overturned at 19 Mile. The owner was located and said people had flipped out of it and the boat was empty, floating downriver.
Sunday, June 5, 2011	Caller reported a fire. An officer responded and found the owner of the property was having a cookout.

Friday, June 10, 2011	Caller reported kids climbing on the trees and onto the roof at the school. Officer responded and found the kids, who did not make it on to the roof and were just trying.
Thursday, June 16, 2011	Caller reported a foul smell coming from the cruise ship and that it smelled like burnt rubber. Officer responded to find that the boat was having engine problems and spewing black smoke.
Friday, June 17, 2011	Caller reported a person passed out in a vehicle. Officer responded and found a man sleeping in his truck between fishing trips. Person was asked to move along, as they were on private property.
Friday, July 7, 2011	Caller reported information about an illegal tour offered without a permit.
Thursday, June 21, 2012	A 911 caller reported a fire. Fire department dispatched but found no signs of fire (Editor's note: it was the SUNRISE).
Tuesday, August 7, 2012	A tour guide reported a pile of six decomposing eagle bodies on the side of the road near Letnikof Cove. F&G were advised and determined the carcasses were, in fact, those of chickens.
Friday, August 9, 2013	A runner found a purse and bright pink running shoes in the middle of the sidewalk in front of a business on Main Street and turned the items in to the police. Dispatch located the owner and the items were returned.
Tuesday, September 17, 2013	2053: A caller requested extra patrol around her home due to trash with food in it. Police advised that this was a bear attractant and citable. The caller moved the food inside the residence.
Tuesday, June 10, 2014	1139: A male was reported to be yelling on the Port Chilkoot dock. Police responded and found the male was only singing to music.

Saturday, August 30, 2014	1533: A 911 caller reported two kite boarders stranded in the water near Pyramid Island. Alaska Mountain Guides and ambulance crew assisted in rescue. There were no injuries.

In recent years, Haines has put together a marching band for the parades held in town, complete with costumes (sometimes), but always with the quintessential Xtra-tufs.

May, 2012: Moose and two calves place their mark on a newly poured sidewalk at 3rd and Main.

Saturday, August 23, 2014: The First Annual Totem Trot in Haines. Participants run or walk 5K along a path that includes 12 totems.

4) AUTUMN

Monday, August 16, 2010	A Front Street resident called requesting a sign to warn of a sharp corner at Front Street and Lutak Road.
Monday, August 16, 2010	Caller came to the police station to say DOT has made Front Street and Lutak Road a traffic hazard.
Tuesday, August 24, 2010	State road crews were advised of a mudslide at 19 Mile Haines Highway.
Sunday, August 29, 2010	Caller reported mud puddles in a business parking lot at 3rd Avenue and Haines Highway were bubbling. The bubbles were caused by an aerating device intended to clean soil of contaminants.
Sunday, August 29, 2010	An officer responded to a request for assistance from a customs officer who was meeting with a questionable person.
Friday, September 3, 2010	A bartender reported a fight was about to start outside a Main Street bar. An officer arrested a Juneau resident who pulled a knife and pursued a local man, but was tackled by others.
Friday, September 3, 2010	Caller reported a truck at the Letnikof boat launch that was submerged to the top of the vehicle. Troopers responded and found the truck had been pulled out of the water.
Saturday, September 4, 2010	Public works reported a water leak on *Soapsuds* Alley (*appropriate name for the circumstance...*).

Wednesday, September 8, 2010	Caller reported a vehicle driving slowly and crossing the center line between 18 Mile and 10 Mile Haines Highway. Police determined they were sightseeing.
Thursday, September 9, 2010	Caller reported they sold a gun to someone three years ago and were not paid for it. They were referred to local court.
Friday, September 10, 2010	Firemen responded to a call that a popcorn machine was on fire inside a Main Street bar.
Sunday, September 12, 2010	A Wasilla caller awaiting shipment of a boat reported a vehicle pulling it was broken down on Lutak Road. Police determined the vehicle was broken down in the Yukon Territory.
Wednesday, September 15, 2010	Caller reported a helicopter flying over their residence. Police determined the flight was a medical emergency.
Friday, September 17, 2010	Caller requested advice about a friend in Juneau who continually phones them when they are sleeping.
Sunday, September 19, 2010	Caller reported a laptop computer stolen from their home at 7 Mile Haines Highway a few months ago. Troopers were advised.
Monday, September 20, 2010	Caller reported a person dancing in the living room of a house owned by a person the dancer was not supposed to be with.
Wednesday, October 13, 2010	Caller reported a car going into a ditch near 5 Mile Haines Highway. An officer who responded found the car had turned onto an access road for a picnic near the river.

Tuesday, October 19, 2010	Caller reported a motel key was not turned in and they needed assistance to find the person who had it (*Editor's note: yes, hotels in Haines use real keys*).
Wednesday, October 20, 2010	Police referred to troopers a caller who wanted a person removed from their boat docked at Letnikof Cove.
Thursday, October 21, 2010	Caller reported a foreclosed home they just purchased had a lock on it. The officer advised they could cut the lock if they owned the house.
Sunday, October 24, 2010	Caller reported finding a gun in the road. An officer determined the caller was in Juneau.
Monday, October 25, 2010	Public works reported a person did road work without permission.
Tuesday, September 6, 2011	Caller reported a skiff sank in the Letnikof Harbor but is still tied to the dock. AST advised.
Tuesday, September 13, 2011	Caller reported there is possibly someone staying in his vacant house that isn't supposed to be there. Officers responded and found evidence of someone possibly staying there. Officers advised the caller to have a friend to close all the windows and lock the doors.
Saturday, September 17, 2011	Caller reported a person outside their downtown house, banging on the door to get in after an argument. The caller then said she reached the person on their cell phone, and no officer response was needed.
Friday, October 28, 2011	Caller reported an unattended fire at Main and Union Streets. An officer responded and said the fire was an attended cooking fire.
Tuesday, August 28, 2012	A borough employee requested extra patrols in an area where grass had been recently seeded.

Sunday, November 25, 2012	A caller reported suspicious circumstances regarding a conversation. The acquaintance had asked when she was not going to be home. The individual requested extra patrols at the residence while she was working. Patrols were conducted but no suspicious activity was observed.
Thursday, November 29, 2012	A chimney fire was reported on Piedad Road. Fire volunteers responded and the fire was put out. Fire responders advised the chimney was very hot and that the caller would be watching it carefully.
Friday, November 30, 2012	Caller requested police check on a vehicle parked in a driveway with its door ajar. Police contacted the owner, who reported the door was broken and would be fixed.
Saturday, December 1, 2012	A chimney fire was reported on Tower Road. Firefighters as well as an officer responded within six minutes and were on-scene for three minutes, as the fire was pretty much extinguished upon their arrival.
Saturday, September 7, 2013	A boat owner couldn't locate his deckhand and called to see if he was in jail. He wasn't.
Saturday, October 5, 2013	0110: Police, harbor staff, volunteer firefighters and many concerned citizens responded to a report of a boat sinking in the Small Boat Harbor. The boat sank and a fuel spill response plan was implemented.The harbor was closed to prevent the spread of fuel.
Saturday, October 5, 2013	1045: Extra patrols are requested by AST to keep an eye on the harbor due to fuel spilled. The caller advised the harbor will be closed until the cleanup is finished.

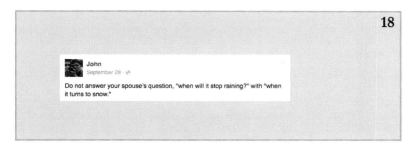

Saturday, November 2, 2013	Caller reported an altercation between two people. Police responded. Investigation revealed the man had kicked several rotten pumpkins around the yard in his frustration. Officers determined no crime had been committed.
Monday, November 4, 2013	Caller reported seeing a minor with a gun on Halloween. The caller said he was dressed up like a soldier. Police advised carrying a gun is not illegal.

Tuesday, September 2, 2014	0820: A caller near Mile 1 Haines Highway reported that it appeared that someone had attempted to break into their shop. HBPD officer responded and met with the caller, whom had found tape on the door frame. The caller was able to confirm the tape had been placed there by an employee. No crime.
Thursday, October 2, 2014	The harbormaster reported a vehicle parked illegally and blocking access to the fuel tanks in the Ice House parking lot. The vehicle prevented filling of the tanks and interfered with the operation of the harbor. The owner of the vehicle was called numerous times by the harbormaster and HBPD dispatch, but without success in making contact. A HBPD officer responded, issued a parking citation and initiated towing of the vehicle for violation of the posted no parking and blocking the fuel tank access. The lot is posted with warnings that violators will be towed at their expense.
Thursday, October 2, 2014	Caller reported hearing a gun shot near the airport. Police investigated and noted that several people had launched a boat to retrieve a moose that they had shot. They were east of the airport at about 3.5 mile along the Highway, but down near the river. The illegal discharge of a firearm in the townsite limits is being investigated.
Friday, October 10, 2014	0751: A caller reported a landslide had closed the road at about 5 mile Lutak Road. DOT was advised and responded.
Monday, November 17, 2014	2235: A resident of Beach Road reported hearing an alarm going off at a business on Beach Road. A HBPD officer responded to the scene and conducted a building sweep. The officer advised that the alarms going off were from smoke detectors. It was determined the batteries had failed as there was no smoke and the batteries were replaced.

Wednesday, November 26, 2014	1616: Fire personnel responded to a dial alarm at the Veteran's Center. The firefighter determined that residents in the building were roasting walnuts and accidentally set off the alarm; there was no fire.
Monday, December 1, 2014	A 911 call was received from a disconnected cell phone. The caller was advised that cell phones with batteries can still call 911 even though they have been disconnected. No emergency.
Monday, December 8, 2014	1335: Haines Police assisted a motorist whose vehicle had slid into the ditch off 3rd Avenue due to icy conditions. Tow services were contacted.

5) WINTER

19

Thursday, January 7, 2010	Caller reported *Soap Suds Alley* was slick and needed gravel on it. Public Works advised.
Tuesday, January 12, 2010	Caller reported a truck pulling two snowboarders with a tow rope on a city street. Officer responded.
Tuesday, January 12, 2010	Caller reported a young child carrying wood into a residence. Officer advised.
Thursday, January 14, 2010	Caller reported their neighbor was pushing snow into their property and they have to pay a snowplow to remove it. Officer responded and the neighbors came to a resolution.

Saturday, January 16, 2010	Caller reported someone had just stolen their snow machine. The caller chased the snow machine down and an officer arrested two suspects who were trying to flee the scene.
Monday, February 1, 2010	Nothing to report on this day.
Tuesday, February 9, 2010	Caller reported a neighbor was pushing snow onto their property with a snowplow so the caller stood in front of the plower and was hit. Caller was unharmed. AST advised.
Monday, February 29, 2010	Caller reported a mud slide across from the ferry terminal. DOT advised.
Thursday, December 30, 2010	Caller reported a forklift slid off 3rd Avenue. An officer responded and blocked traffic so the forklift could be pulled out of a snowbank.
Monday, January 3, 2011	Caller reported two people screaming at each other on Main Street. An officer responded and found two intoxicated males arguing about how to get back to their accommodations. They were given a ride to their destination.
Tuesday, January 11, 2011	Caller reported the Alcan 200 sign hanging above Main Street had blown down part way and could be a driving hazard. Officer responded.
Wednesday, January 12, 2011	Motel owners were contacted when an officer found their metal roofing was about to blow off at 1 Mile Haines Highway.
Saturday, January 15, 2011	A person brought in a street sign that was found blowing down the road. Public works advised.
Friday, January 21, 2011	Caller requested assistance for a building they own that was reported to have water around it. Assistance given.

Friday, January 21, 2011	Caller reported a large, water filled pot hole at 3 Mile Haines Highway that could be a driving hazard. DOT advised.
Friday, January 21, 2011	Road crews were advised a four-way stop downtown was icy and needed sand.
Friday, January 21, 2011	Caller reported a power line on 4th Avenue was snapping loudly and throwing sparks. Alaska Power and Telephone was advised.
Saturday January 22, 2011	Caller reported a broken water line by a local business. Public Works advised.
Saturday January 22, 2011	Caller reported a tree down across Front Street. DOT advised.
Saturday January 22, 2011	Caller reported the intersection of Allen and Menaker was icy and they slid sideways. DOT advised.
Saturday January 22, 2011	Caller reported Piedad Road was icy and they were unable to stop at the stop sign at the bottom of the hill. DOT advised.
Saturday January 22, 2011	Caller reported Mud Bay Road and Mount Riley hill were icy. DOT advised.
Saturday January 22, 2011	Caller reported Cemetery Hill had several cars off the road because it was icy. Officer responded.
Saturday January 22, 2011	Caller reported a stop sign down at Battle Road. Public Works advised.
Sunday, January 23, 2011	Officer discovered a cabin at 4.5 mile Haines Highway that had an unsecured door due to weather damage.
Tuesday, January 25, 2011	Caller reported a person continuously knocking on their door in the middle of the night. Officer responded and took the knocker to a motel.

Sunday, January 30, 2011	Caller reported a large hole of ice on Beach Road which could be a driving hazard. Public Works responded.
Tuesday, February 8, 2011	Received a report that Beach Road near Portage Cove Campground was a solid sheet of ice. DOT advised and responded.
Monday, February 14, 2011	Caller reported their vehicle was stuck in on Mud Bay because of high snow drifts. Officer responded.
Saturday, February 19, 2011	Caller reported 12 inches of snow on Haines Highway between the airport and 10 Mile. DOT advised.
Tuesday, February 22, 2011	Caller reported snow machines tailgating them and passing on the right side of the lane. Officer contacted the juvenile drivers and informed them of requirements for snow machines on the roadway.
Friday, February 25, 2011	Caller reported unusual footprints around their home that went under the bedroom window. Officer responded and said the footprints were connected with an earlier accident on upper Young Road when officers were trying to locate the driver.
Sunday, February 27, 2011	Caller reported a $200.00 robe was missing from the closet at the Chilkat Center. Officer advised.

Monday, February 28, 2011	Caller reported evidence of someone sleeping overnight at the Chilkat Center. Officer advised.
Monday, February 28, 2011	Caller requested police assistance in asking people not to push snow into their rose bushes downtown. Officer advised.
Wednesday, March 16, 2011	Caller reported he was run off of the road by another vehicle on 2nd and Haines Highway. Officer advised and said ice was a factor.
Saturday, March 19, 2011	A caller reported that a carbon monoxide monitor was beeping in his home. A fireman responded and determined it had been set off by a car running in the garage and wind blowing the fumes into the house.
Sunday, March 27, 2011	Caller reported suspicious people messing around with a boat by the ferry terminal. An officer responded and found the boat owners were preparing their boat for transport.
Wednesday, November 9, 2011	Caller reported black smoke coming from a burn barrel. Fireman responded and found the barrel barely smoking.
Saturday, November 12, 2011	Caller reported a vehicle in the ditch around a bad corner and blocking part of a lane. AST advised and message was left on the vehicle owner's phone.
Monday, November 14, 2011	Caller reported unsafe road conditions on the 3rd Avenue hill. Police blocked off the road until it could be sanded.
Wednesday, November 23, 2011	Citizen came in to test their level on the Datamaster (breath alcohol level). Officer assisted and found them too intoxicated to drive.

Saturday, November 26, 2011	Caller reported a snowplow threw snow onto their property and caused damage to a tent. Officer and DOT advised.
Wednesday, January 11, 2012	Caller reported their vehicle sustained damage that occurred during the night while parked at their downtown residence. Police said another vehicle likely ran into it after sliding on ice. Officer initiated a case.
Friday, January 13, 2012	Caller reported fuel oil had been siphoned from a tank in the FAA Road area, but police determined the tank had been damaged by snow falling off the roof and the fuel oil had leaked out.
Friday, January 13, 2012	A snowplow operator reported striking a junk vehicle that had been abandoned on Deishu Drive. Officer responded.
Monday, January 16, 2012	A 4th Avenue caller was concerned about intruders after the front door of their residence opened and closed. Police responded and found nothing out of the ordinary and advised the wind had most likely been the culprit.
Saturday, January 21, 2012	A caller reported someone was in violation of conditions of release and was drinking in a downtown bar. Police could not verify the complaint, because all the bars were closed.
Sunday, January 22, 2012	Several motorists were assisted in getting home by police, as the roads were impeded with heavy snowfall.
Monday, January 23, 2012	Two vehicles were impeding snow removal near the area of the power plant.
Thursday, January 26, 2012	A resident complained about being plowed in and was advised not to park on the roadway or his vehicle would be towed.

Friday, January 27, 2012	Caller reported a residence on Front Street had a porch collapse under a load of snow.
Monday, January 30, 2012	A 911 caller reported a suspicious light at a basement of a residence. It was later determined to be an indicator light indicating the tank is out of fuel.
Monday, January 30, 2012	Caller reported he had a warrant out of Florida for violation of his probation. Florida Department of Corrections was contacted and will not extradite. Caller had no place to stay and was assisted by a local church who will assist with transportation to Juneau.
Tuesday, January 31, 2012	Officers responded to several vehicles parked during snow removal resulting in three issued citations for vehicles obstructing snow removal.
Thursday, February 2, 2012	There was one traffic stop for erratic driving. Officer determined the driver had snow on the windshield and not able to observe the road.
Friday, February 3, 2012	Caller reported a damaged window from attempted forced entry on Main Street. Police said the damage might have been due to snow or a break-in attempt.
Saturday, February 11, 2012	An officer assisted a motorist with minor automobile repair.
Wednesday, February 15, 2012	A local business requested extra patrols due to a garage door that would not shut.
Saturday, February 18, 2012	Caller reported a vehicle accident with a jack-knifed truck and trailer with logs at the intersection of Mathias and Young Roads which blocked access to the road.

Monday, February 20, 2012	Caller reported an altercation near a 2nd Avenue business. It was determined this was a sibling argument while on their way to school.
Sunday, February 26, 2012	Caller reported electrical current running through a pedestrian ramp at the Post Office. A supervisor at that facility was informed. It was determined there was no current there.
Friday, March 23, 2012	Caller reported that someone had cut a tree on her property without her permission. Later, the caller indicated that she had been in error regarding property boundaries, and the tree was not on her property.
Monday, March 26, 2012	Caller reported hearing people yelling possibly involving a cat near their residence behind Deishu. Officer checked the area and determined it was most likely the firemen in training behind the fire hall.
Friday, March 30, 2012	Caller reported the return of the propane tank previously reported stolen from Haines Propane.
Tuesday, October 2, 2012	Caller reported a propane tank had been stolen from the garage of a residence. The tank was later determined to have been borrowed by a friend.
Saturday, November 11, 2012	An anonymous caller reported a vehicle accident near the intersection of 3rd Avenue and Main Street. A parked vehicle had popped out of gear and rolled through the intersection, coming to rest near a picnic table. No damages or injuries were reported, and no citation was issued.

Tuesday, November 20, 2012	The building owner of a Fort Seward business reported a man drove his vehicle into the side of the structure. The vehicle had slid on the ice, hit the building, and cracked a wall of the structure. Police investigated and initiated a case. The driver was not cited.
Thursday, November 29, 2012	A local restaurant and bar owner requested information on assisting a homeless male who is currently sleeping in a tent and who was asking about places to live in her restaurant. Police have previously attempted to provide assistance to the male but he has refused. The complainant was told that the male could contact Salvation Army if he needs assistance and that if he wishes to sleep in a tent that is his choice.
Sunday, December 2, 2012	An officer reported a vehicle parked in the middle of 2nd Avenue. The owner said he left the car there because he thought it could not make it up Young Road. The owner moved the vehicle.
Friday, December 7, 2012	A caller requested ministerial association assistance to stay in a motel due to toxic odors in her home. The caller had used an over-the-counter cleaner to address plumbing issues and reported the fumes were causing shortness of breath.
Friday, December 7, 2012	A caller reported ongoing thefts from the wood supply at her residence. Officers advised the woman install a motion-activated alarm or light.
Saturday, December 8, 2012	A three-vehicle accident was reported on Main Street and 3rd Avenue. One vehicle slid through a stop sign and struck another vehicle, which spun into a third vehicle. One was towed from the scene. No injuries were reported.

Sunday, December 9, 2012	Caller reported an assault on FAA Road. An officer contacted the alleged victim who said an individual had slapped her hands and knocked her cell phone down during an argument over a snow blower. Both parties were urged to avoid one another, if possible.
Wednesday, December 19, 2012	Caller complained of snow berms being deliberately deposited in front of a business driveway. She was advised that the plows do not clear berms from driveways.
Saturday, December 22, 2012	Two vehicles were reported broken down on 3rd Avenue and Haines Highway. One vehicle had stopped to help the other and both moved on. Officers advised.
Friday, December 28, 2012	A woman reported observing unusual lights in the sky over Fort Seward the night before. An officer on patrol had seen similar strange lights and upon investigating learned people were releasing Chinese lanterns.
Sunday, December 30, 2012	An anonymous caller reported a juvenile female's intention of attending a drinking party with her boyfriend and no chaperone. The caller could not provide a location.
Wednesday, January 2, 2013	A caller in the Highland Drive and Muncaster Road area reported a constant low hum. Police determined the noise to be a neighbor's lights.
Saturday, January 5, 2013	An earthquake was felt in Haines and a Tsunami warning issued for the Southeast Alaska coastline. The earthquake was reported as a 7.7 on the Richter scale and later as a 7.6. .The assistant harbormaster and fire chief went down to the harbor to observe wave activity. The Tsunami warning was cancelled shortly after.

Monday, January 7, 2013	A Small Tracts Road resident reported loud noises sounding like something being ripped apart on his property. Police responded and found this to be the neighboring business using a backhoe.
Monday, January 7, 2013	Caller reported seeing a truck do a "donut" and then slide off to the side of 2nd Avenue partly on to the sidewalk. It was determined to have been a parked car that slid on the ice. The owner was made aware of the situation and attended to the vehicle.
Monday, January 7, 2013	Caller reported a flashlight-wielding intruder in an absent neighbor's home in the Young Road area. Police responded and concluded an authorized yoga class was occurring and the neighbor had seen someone wearing a headlamp.
Thursday, January 10, 2013	Caller reported her car had slid on the ice, hit a snow berm and overturned near 1.5 Mile Haines Highway. She sustained no injuries and was assisted in getting out of the vehicle by a city plow driver.
Saturday, January 12, 2013	HBPD assisted a business when an individual reported an odd smell coming from the maintenance shed. An officer responded and found a piece of recently burned PVC pipe near a Toyo stove. Dispatch contacted the business responsible.
Tuesday, January 15, 2013	A school employee in Mosquito Lake school advised the roads were very icy in that area and requested that the high school bus be advised. DOT was aware of the issue and were already sanding roads.

50

Thursday, January 17, 2013	The harbormaster reported being threatened by a man who was told he could not live on his boat during winter. Police responded and attempted to locate the man but did not make contact until the following day. Charges of assault in the fourth degree are being forwarded to the district attorney's office.
Saturday, January 19, 2013	A passing motorist reported a disoriented male walking from 2nd Avenue to Haines Highway. Officers located the man in front of the police station and concluded he was an elderly person who does not walk very often.
Sunday, January 20, 2013	A resident reported hearing high-powered rifle shots coming from across the water in the Beach Road area. The caller was advised there is a shooting range in that area. An officer responded and found nothing suspicious.
Monday, January 21, 2013	Several callers reported that a grader hit a phone pole and power went out in the Deishu area. Alaska Power & Telephone responded.
Wednesday, January 23, 2013	Police served a trespass order on behalf of the borough to a male who had been on the Borough Harbor Property unlawfully. The man had been living on his boat during the winter.
Thursday, January 24, 2013	A woman on Haines Highway reported her boyfriend had deliberately rammed her vehicle from behind while she was driving home. She was referred to troopers and assured that she was in a safe place for the night.
Thursday, January 31, 2013	A man requested ministerial services for a month of housing. Ministerial services reported they are unable to fund that much and advised they would provide transport to Juneau only.

Friday, February 1, 2013	Police received report of a vehicle theft. Officers, AST, Canadian Customs and the ferry terminal were advised. The owner found the vehicle in a ditch at Fort Seward.
Friday, February 8, 2013	A borough employee reported a vehicle parked for a week at the dock apparently broken down. A relative of the vehicle owner reported the owners were on a canoe trip and the vehicle was not broken down.
Thursday, February 14, 2013	A woman sought help securing shelter for a few days while awaiting the ferry. Ministerial Services assisted.
Saturday, February 16, 2013	A complaint was received by an individual who broke her finger when trying to calm down an intoxicated person three nights prior.
Sunday, March 3, 2013	An officer advised dispatch of a rock slide at 2 Mile Lutak Road. The officer cleared the road as much as possible. DOT was notified.
Friday, April 12, 2013	A local guide company reported a snow avalanche and requested ambulance to stand by until all people were recovered. Parties were immediately reported as all recovered and no injuries.
Saturday, April 13, 2013	Dispatch received a call that fireworks were going to be set off for a celebration of life ceremony. Immediately after, phone calls were received from concerned citizens.
Friday, April 26, 2013	A single-vehicle accident at 2.5 Mile Lutak Road resulted in no injuries but major damage to the vehicle. The driver lost control of the vehicle on the slick roads, bounced off the guardrail, and collided with the rock wall. Fire, ambulance and police responded.

Friday, May 10, 2013	1800: A snow slide was reported as being in progress, but slow, at 18 Mile Haines Highway. DOT was advised.
Friday, November 1, 2013	A person reported witnessed an escalating domestic dispute near the intersection of Main Street and 2nd Avenue. A woman was dragging a man, who was clinging to her while she repeatedly knocked him in the head. Police responded and determined no crime had been committed.
Friday, November 1, 2013	A 911 caller reported a domestic dispute on Mud Bay Road. The woman reported the man had grown angry and thrown cupcakes she had baked across the room. No arrests were made and the two were separated for the night.
Saturday, November 9, 2013	0403: A resident reported children screaming on Front Street. An officer responded and discovered young adults yelling at the northern lights. They said they were told that yelling at the lights "makes them react and dance more." The officer told them to keep it down. Northern lights (aurora borealis)

Sunday, March 9, 2014 --- *this is after 15"* *snowfall*	0651: A caller reported being trapped in the cabin of his boat at the Small Boat Harbor due to the amount of snowfall. The harbormaster was advised and assisted. The caller couldn't open his hatch due to the amount of snow on his deck.
Sunday, December 7, 2014	A caller reported his vehicle slide through *the* 4-way stop at 2nd Avenue and Main Street due to ice. DOT was advised (*Editor's note: there is only one 4-way stop in the townsite of Haines, and no stoplights*).
Sunday, December 7, 2014	A caller reported the Highway was slippery with black ice from *Mile 44 to Mile 3*. DOT was advised.
Monday, December 8, 2014	A resident of Skyline Road called to report her van had been involved in a slide off while coming down from the top of Skyline. There were no injuries reported and the caller advised she was waiting for Bigfoot (Auto) to open to call for a tow. HBPD officer advised.

6) EXAMPLES OF HPD HELPING

Saturday, January 22, 2010	An officer responded to a call from a person who said they were lost downtown.
Monday, January 3, 2011	Caller reported two people screaming at each other. Officer responded and found two intoxicated males arguing about how to get back to their accommodations. They were given a ride to their destination.
Sunday, April 24, 2011	An intoxicated man came to the police station to say he didn't know where he was staying. An officer helped the man find his room at a local bed and breakfast.
Monday, June 20, 2011	A caller requested police help because she was unfamiliar with the area. The caller stated she was camping in town and could not find her friends or the campsite. An officer responded and helped the woman locate the campsite.
Friday, April 27, 2012	An officer made a traffic stop and helped the driver bring the vehicle's taillights into compliance.
Sunday, November 11, 2012	0230: An intoxicated person came to the police station because he missed his ride and had no other way to get to his residence. An officer responded and advised the individual that he is unable to put him in jail but would be able to help give him a ride to his residence.
Thursday, October 18, 2012	Police made contact with a foreign visitor at the ferry terminal. The man was attempting to understand the ferry schedule and police assisted.

Thursday, February 14, 2013	A library employee requested police assistance in helping to locate the home of an out-of-town visitor who was unsure of the location. Police assisted and escorted the man to the residence.
Wednesday, May 8, 2013	Police assisted troopers in service of a felony arrest warrant on a man near Mud Bay Road. The suspect was wanted for aggravated murder in Utah and will be extradited.
Wednesday, May 15, 2013	2030: A 911 caller requested assistance in getting an elderly relative safely inside their residence. Police responded and assisted.
Saturday, May 25, 2013	2317: A report made by a downtown hotel worker advised dispatch that a female went into someone else's room and wouldn't leave. Officers responded and the woman was taken to her room where her friends would take care of her for the night.
Monday, December 8, 2014	Haines Police assisted a motorist whose vehicle had slid into the ditch off 3rd Avenue due to icy conditions. Tow services were contacted.

7) CHECK WELFARE OF PEOPLE

Thursday, December 30, 2010	Caller reported their father had not made it to their residence in Anchorage and the last place they communicated was when the father was in Haines. Customs and AST advised.
Friday, May 20, 2011	Caller reported two individuals went out on a boat to check shrimp pots late at night and no one has heard from them. AST advised. Officer made contact with the two individuals, who had landed their boat between the Port Chilkoot Dock and the boat harbor due to a dead battery.
Monday, May 23, 2011	Caller requested a welfare check on an individual they had not heard from in a week. Officer responded to find no one at home. Dispatch called the ferry terminal who stated the individual had left on a ferry a couple days earlier and would not be home until early June.
Monday, June 27, 2011	Caller requesting a welfare check on their father, whom they have not spoken to in over a year. Officers made contact with the individual, who stated they would call their son.
Wednesday, July 27, 2011	Caller requesting a welfare check on a friend they hadn't heard from in a couple days. Caller soon called back to state the person was in Fairbanks.

Wednesday, July 27, 2011	Caller requesting a welfare check on an older individual who has made several calls to them in the middle of the night and then just hung up. Officer responded to the individual's house.
Thursday, September 15, 2011	Caller requested an officer check to see if their friend's plane was at the airport, as they were supposed to fly into Haines a few days ago and haven't checked in yet. Officers responded and located the plane.
Friday, September 16, 2011	Caller reported two overdue hunters out the Haines Highway. AST advised, and the hunters were found the next morning.
Thursday, January 19, 2012	Caller was concerned they could not get in touch with a family member at a Main Street business, but declined officer assistance.
Wednesday, February 15, 2012	A helicopter flying from Canada to Haines was reported overdue; it was determined the aircraft landed safely in Canada.
Tuesday, March 27, 2012	A relative was concerned a family member from Haines did not arrive on the ferry to Juneau. Contact was made with the family member and advised they had arranged other transportation.
Friday, April 20, 2012	An out-of-town caller requested a welfare check for her parents. Dispatch determined that the parents were okay, just traveling, and advised the caller.
Friday, July 13, 2012	Caller reported a missing juvenile. The youth was located and was safe (the youth was at the fairgrounds and had forgotten to phone home).
Monday, July 23, 2012	Caller requested a welfare check on a relative. Police were unable to locate the woman, who later called the station to say she was okay.

Friday, December 7, 2012	A concerned parent from Minnesota reported hearing an argument between her son and his wife over the phone. She was unable to provide further information or location of the parties.
Monday, December 10, 2012	A caller requested a welfare check on her daughter who was driving to Klukwan in bad road conditions; she was given the AST after-hours number. She later called back and stated her daughter contacted her.
Monday, December 10, 2012	An out of state caller requested assistance contacting a relative at Mosquito Lake. Dispatch provided the caller with the after-hours AST number.
Tuesday, December 18, 2012	A concerned parent requested a welfare check on her daughter who had not shown up at school. Police made contact with the father and the daughter who was fine, but had stayed home sick.
Tuesday, December 18, 2012	A ministerial adviser requested a welfare check on a client who did not answer the door. Police made contact with the client who had been in the shower and was upset, but fine otherwise.
Friday, February 8, 2013	An out-of-state caller requested a welfare check on a man who had not been answering his phone. The welfare check was conducted and found the male to have been sleeping and confirmed he would contact his family.
Saturday, February 9, 2013	A family member requested a welfare check on an individual who was possibly drinking heavily. Officers arrived and requested an ambulance for high intoxication.

Thursday, March 28, 2013	A male requested a welfare check on his daughter who had not been answering his phone calls and he expressed concern for unauthorized persons at the residence. Police found no one at the home and the daughter's vehicle was located elsewhere. The caller was advised.
Thursday, May 9, 2013	An overdue aircraft was reported as having not closed the flight plan. Police determined there was a communication error and the plane had landed in Haines as planned and the flight plan was closed by the pilot after contact was made.
Saturday, May 18, 2013	1230: Caller requested a welfare check on a female in Haines. The female was contacted and stated she was fine and stated that the caller needed to cease calling as it was causing domestic problems.
Monday, June 17, 2013	1500: Dispatch received a report of a paddle boarder that was out in the water near the Port Chilkoot dock. The caller was concerned because the wind picked up and they were unable to spot them. HPD and AST searched the area but were unable to locate the paddle boarder. U.S. Coast Guard was also advised.
Friday, July 25, 2014	Caller requested a welfare check on an elderly woman living in the area of Barnett Drive. The caller believed the woman's phone was off the hook. An officer checked on the woman and found her to be fine and the phone off the hook.

8) LOCK OUT OF CAR OR HOUSE

Thursday, January 7, 2010	Caller reported a vehicle stuck in gear on the side of the road with two dogs locked inside. Officer responded and AST advised.
Wednesday, January 26, 2011	Caller reported being locked out of their vehicle when their dog hit the locks from the inside. Officer responded.
Sunday, May 8, 2011	Caller reported they had been locked out of their car. Officer responded in an attempt to help the driver find the Hide-a-Key but was unable to find it. When the officer went to find someone with a key the driver was able to locate the key and leave the area.
Thursday, May 19, 2011	Caller reported their boyfriend had taken the keys to her car and threw them. The caller was concerned because she might not be able to find them. Caller advised the police station about an hour later that she found the keys locked in her vehicle. Dispatch advised the caller of where they could call in the morning to unlock the car.
Monday, August 1, 2011	Caller reported locking their small child in the car. Officer responded and they found someone with a key.
Monday, February 13, 2012	A caller reported a dog inside a person's vehicle locked the doors. The caller was able to assist with providing a phone number to the victim for assistance.
Thursday, August 30, 2012	A citizen requested assistance with a car lockout. He was locked out of his car by a puppy inside. The man was directed to businesses in town capable of assisting.

Thursday, December 6, 2012	0230: A woman on Helms Loop called 911 for assistance in getting into her house. She had lost her keys and had been trying to enter the house for about three hours. Police responded and as there was no access to the home contacted the Ministerial Services to assist with lodging the woman at a local hotel for the night.
Wednesday, December 19, 2012	Police assisted a female driver at the Post Office parking lot whose locks and doors were frozen shut on her vehicle with the engine running.
Wednesday, January 9, 2013	A woman locked herself out of a running car in the Post Office parking lot and walked to the station to request assistance. Dispatch assisted in contacting a family member to bring a spare key.
Monday, September 22, 2014	1600: A HBPD officer reported a vehicle left running in the roadway on Lynn View. Contact was made at the residence and the vehicle owners advised that they had forgotten the vehicle was still running.
Saturday, October 25, 2014	A resident on Helms Loop called to report a window on her residence appears to have been tampered with and removed. A HBPD officer made contact and the resident advised the perpetrator had been her nephew, whom lives at the residence. He forgot his key.
Sunday, October 26, 2014	1120: A roadside assistance call was received advising a client/motorist was locked out of her car. The car was running and her toddler was inside. A HBPD officer responded to assist and found no toddler but two small dogs. The officer assisted in unlocking the vehicle.

KHNS-fm
7 hrs · 🔁

From KHNS News: Watch out for a mama bear and cubs. One her three cubs was recently killed by another bear and she's on the defensive. She was spotted near the landfill, and maybe near the fairgrounds and Lutak Road as well.

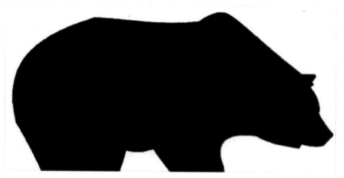

Officials warn of defensive brown bear in Haines area

The Alaska Department of Fish and Game and Haines Borough Police on Thursday warned Haines residents that a brown bear sow in the area was reported being defensive and aggressive

KHNS.ORG

9) ANIMALS

BEARS	
Monday, March 22, 2010	Caller reported a bear has been leaving Haines Sanitation and walking down FAA Road every day for the last week. Officer advised.
Saturday, August 14, 2010	Police traced multiple calls about fireworks being shot off on Comstock Road to a resident who said they were trying to scare off a large bear.
Sunday, August 15, 2010	Caller reported two bears walking into town near the police station.

Sunday, August 15, 2010	Caller reported a bear in a tree at 1st Avenue and Dalton Street.
Friday, August 27, 2010	Caller on Small Tracts Road near the storage-rental business reported that at 3:00 p.m. August 26 they had twice shot a bear that was eating their chickens. Troopers were unable to locate the bear.
Monday, August 30, 2010	Public works was advised that a bear ripped open the trash bin at Oslund Park softball field and trash was everywhere.
Tuesday, August 31, 2010	Caller reported a bear ripped off the side mirror of a car on Tower Road while they were out of town.
Friday, September 3, 2010	An officer chased off three bears that were getting into a cherry tree at a Small Tracts Road residence.
Saturday, September 4, 2010	Caller reported a bear had destroyed their apple tree on Small Tracts Road.
Saturday, September 4, 2010	Caller reported a bear got into their enclosed porch at Officer's Row and did $2,000 damage.
Saturday, September 4, 2010	Caller reported a dog chased two bears onto a porch on Tower Road.
Sunday, September 5, 2010	A pedestrian requested a courtesy ride after seeing two bears walking up 4th Avenue.
Sunday, September 5, 2010	2330: Caller reported a bear on Main Street heading up 1st Avenue. An officer found two bears and chased them into the woods after shooting one with a Taser.

Monday, September 6, 2010	0230: Caller reported two bears walking up 2nd Avenue, north of Main Street. Officer responded and found the bears had gotten into the bank trash can and a dumpster in a nearby alley. Officer chased them into the woods near 4th Avenue.
Monday, September 6, 2010	0245: Caller reported two bears on 3rd Avenue, south of Main Street. An officer found the same, black-colored sow and cub from earlier calls and chased them into the woods by Haines Highway.
Wednesday, September 8, 2010	Caller reported a bear broke into a locked, wooden shed on Tower Road. A responding officer chased off the bear, then chased it off again when it returned a half hour later.
Tuesday, September 14, 2010	An officer gave a ride to a pedestrian who saw a bear at the Halsingland Hotel on their walk home.
Tuesday, October 12, 2010	Caller reported a bear pulled a small, wooden shed into FAA Road behind Officer's Row.
Tuesday, October 12, 2010	A bear was reported at the Dusty Trails apartments multiple times during the night.
Thursday, October 14, 2010	Caller reported a bear pushing over a dumpster at the Dusty Trails apartment complex.
Saturday, October 16, 2010	A person brought in a bullet that was found in bear meat they received, believing it was an exploding copper slug. It wasn't.
Saturday, October 23, 2010	Caller reported a bear had gotten into the school trash.

Saturday, October 23, 2010	An officer responded when caller requested extra police patrols at the school because a bear had been seen in the area, and students were there at night for a dance.
Sunday, February 13, 2011	Caller reported a young black bear alongside Haines Highway that appeared to be lost. Officer and AST responded but could not locate the bear.
Thursday, May 5, 2011	Officer delivered a bear attractant trash warning to a local resident who had garbage loose in their yard.
Saturday, May 21, 2011	Caller reported some sort of carcass was in the river at the 4 Mile Haines Highway pull off. Caller stated there were a lot of eagles eating on it but she could not identify the species of the carcass. AST advised, who found the remains of a harvested bear.
Saturday, June 18, 2011	Person reported a nuisance bear in their neighborhood on Otter Lane. Person reported the bear has eaten their barbecue and has jumped up and looked in the back windows of their house. Officer advised.
Tuesday, July 12, 2011	Caller reported a bear had gotten into his burn barrel on Small Tracts Road.

Saturday, July 16, 2011	Caller reported a bear broke into their vehicle on Mud Bay Road and ate a loaf of bread several days ago.
Saturday, July 16, 2011	Caller reported a bear had gotten into the canopy of his truck and taken two garbage cans out of it.
Friday, July 22, 2011	Caller reported a bear broke into their car the night before and pulled out several water jugs. The caller stated she had a salmon skin in the front seat that may have attracted the bear. The caller also stated her neighbor's smoker had been torn into and the other neighbor's trash was strewn around.
Saturday, July 23, 2011	Officers found a mother bear with two cubs at the waterfront along Beach Road and tried to get them to go into the woods.
Friday, July 29, 2011	Caller reported a white Dodge pickup swerving on the way into town from Lutak. Officer made contact with the individual who was watching bears on the drive in from Lutak.
Monday, August 8, 2011	Caller on Helms Loop Road reported sometime in the last day a bear broke out the windows on their garage and scratched the side of their truck.
Monday, August 8, 2011	Caller on Helms Loop Road reported a bear tore off the screens to their porch.
Friday, August 12, 2011	Police found a bear had tried to get into a hangar at the airport. Police advised the hangar owner.
Sunday, August 14, 2011	An officer and a park ranger responded to a call about people crowding bears along the Chilkoot River.

Sunday, August 14, 2011	Caller reported someone dumped about a dozen pink salmon by the Oslund Park baseball fields. An officer put the fish in a bear-proof dumpster there.
Monday, August 15, 2011	Caller reported a bear cub at Chilkoot River with a fishhook stuck in its nose.
Tuesday, August 16, 2011	A water plant worker reported a bear tried to enter the FAA Road building and ripped up several bags of chemicals.

Thursday, August 18, 2011	Caller sought a ride home after they saw a bear walk across Small Tracts Road in front of them. An officer drove the person home.
Monday, August 22, 2011	Caller said a bear was getting into their neighbor's cherry trees on 1st Avenue. There had been another call for a bear at the same residence on August 18.
Saturday, August 27, 2011	Caller reported a black bear had been shocked several times by an electric fence surrounding a chicken coop near 1 Mile Mud Bay Road. An officer responded and the bear ran off into an unpopulated area.
Saturday, August 27, 2011	Caller reported hitting a small black bear at 2 Mile Lutak Road. An officer and park ranger responded and located the dead bear, and a wildlife trooper disposed of it.
Sunday, August 28, 2011	A business reported a bear got into their dumpster on 6th Avenue and Union Street. An officer responded and said the business did not violate the Haines Borough's bear attraction nuisance ordinance, because the dumpster had been chained shut.
Sunday, August 28, 2011	Caller reported a bear eating berries next to the track at the school. Officers responded and ran the bear away.
Sunday, August 28, 2011	Caller reported a bear trying to break into their garage on FAA Road.
Monday, August 29, 2011	A business reported a bear caused about $4,000 in damage to a construction site near the Southeast Alaska State Fairgrounds. Another business reported a bear caused about $400 in damage to a shop door at 1 Mile Haines Highway.

Monday, August 29, 2011	Callers reported a bear walking around downtown. An officer responded and did not locate the bear.
Monday, August 29, 2011	Caller reported a bear walking across Main Street toward the track. State troopers were advised, and the bear went into the wooded area across from the school.
Monday, August 29, 2011	Caller reported a bear pushing on the side of their downtown apartment.
Tuesday, August 30, 2011	Caller reported a bear walking from the Fish and Game building toward the school.
Tuesday, August 30, 2011	The school reported a bear had walked into the woods in front of the school.
Tuesday, August 30, 2011	A person reported a bear crossing the street at 2nd Avenue and heading toward the Senior Center.
Tuesday, August 30, 2011	An officer found the speed radar trailer had been knocked over by a bear.
Tuesday, August 30, 2011	Caller reported a bear on the track at the school. An officer responded and was unable to scare off the bear, but determined it was not a threat.
Tuesday, August 30, 2011	Caller reported a bear at their window. Officer responded.
Thursday, September 1, 2011	Caller reported their dog chased a bear up a tree on Front Street. Officers responded and scared the bear into the woods.
Thursday, September 1, 2011	Caller reported a bear near the school. School officials were told to advise students.

Saturday, September 3, 2011	Multiple callers reported a bear breaking into garages and eventually breaking down a basement door. The bear was dispatched and placed in the morgue until AST could take care of it.
Sunday, September 4, 2011	Caller reported finding a cooler full of fish on Front Street and a bear was eating out of it. Officer advised.
Thursday, September 8, 2011	Caller reported hearing three gunshots from a neighbor's house the previous night. Officers made contact with the individuals who shot over a bears head to chase it away. The residence was advised to call the police station if they have a bear problem and to not fire a gun in city limits.
Tuesday, September 20, 2011	Caller reported a sow with two cubs is bedding down in their driveway. Officer advised.
Wednesday, September 21, 2011	The landfill reported a large brown bear wandering around. Officer advised.
Wednesday, September 21, 2011	Caller reported a bear cub has been hit by a car and left. Officer responded and a charity was called to pick up the bear.
Wednesday, September 21, 2011	Caller reported a bear on their porch getting into their trash. Officers responded.
Thursday, September 22, 2011	Caller reported their dog just got attacked by a bear. Officer responded. The dog had minor injuries.
Friday, September 23, 2011	The landfill reported a problem bear that will not leave. Officer responded.
Friday, September 23, 2011	Caller reporting a black bear in a tree on Front Street. Officer advised.

Saturday, October 1, 2011	Person reporting damage to their car. Officer responded and found evidence that it was caused by a bear.
Saturday, November 12, 2011	Caller reported an apparently abandoned bear cub at 21 Mile Haines Highway. AST advised.
Wednesday, May 16, 2012	A residence advised three bears were in their yard. Officer responded and shot two bears with rubber slugs, and all the bears left.
Friday, May 25, 2012	Caller reported two bears and a moose on her property and that one of the bears chased the moose in the direction of Small Tracts Road. Officer responded and searched the area without further contact with bears or moose.
Tuesday, May 29, 2012	A bear was reported to have broken into a freezer, stolen a package of hash browns and damaged a Beach Road property. Officer responded and advised owners to contact F&G.
Wednesday, May 30, 2012	A menacing bear was reported to be back in the area of Beach Road and had broke into two garages. An officer responded and determined the bear had also torn open a shed and chomped on a charcoal grill. The bear was shot with three rubber slugs and wandered off. The bear was reported back in the area later in the day but an officer was unable to locate it.
Thursday, May 31, 2012	A bear threatening goats was shot by the owner. Officer responded, filed a report and notified AST.
Saturday, June 9, 2012	Caller complained that people stopping to photograph bear cubs at 2 Mile Lutak Road were creating a traffic hazard.
Thursday, June 28, 2012	A bear was reported in a yard on Lynn View Drive but had jumped over a fence before police arrived.

Saturday, June 30, 2012	A caller reported a bear in a neighbor's yard on Mud Bay Road tearing up a cardboard box and dragging coolers into the woods. Officer responded and scared the bear off with rubber bullets.
Friday, July 6, 2012	Caller reported a bear damaged an unoccupied travel trailer.
Saturday, July 7, 2012	Caller reported a bear scattering trash on Barnett Drive.
Monday, July 9, 2012	A bear was reported at 1 Mile Lutak Road and had caused damage to buckets and a kiddie pool.
Tuesday, July 10, 2012	A caller in the West Fair Drive area reported a bear had gotten into a grill and was reluctant to leave the property when the dog intervened and "bear bangers" were used. The caller brought the grill into a garage.
Wednesday, July 11, 2012	A brown bear was reported getting into the neighbor's shed and eating something near FAA Road. Officers responded and shot it with a beanbag round and the bear left into the woods. The owner of the shed was verbally warned for bear attractant.
Wednesday, July 11, 2012	A bear was reported sitting on a porch at a residence on Matrix Road, then moved to the lawn. The caller was advised to leave the bear alone and call back if it caused any damage.
Tuesday, July 17, 2012	Caller reported an employee at a sanitation company had to dispatch a bear for defense of life and property. F&G was advised.
Tuesday, July 24, 2012	Caller reported tourists and dogs were too close to bears at Chilkoot Lake. AST advised and an officer responded.

Wednesday, July 25, 2012	Caller reported a bear in the downtown area between a bar at the harbor and an RV park.
Saturday, July 28, 2012	A bear was reported heading from the Post Office to Port Chilkoot and a number of pedestrians. Police were able to shoot beanbag rounds and chase the bear out toward Lutak Inlet where it appeared to remain away from campers.
Friday, August 17, 2012	An officer deployed a "flash-bang" on Front Street to scare off a bear.
Sunday, August 19, 2012	Caller on FAA Road reported a bear attempted to break into his smokehouse.
Thursday, August 30, 2012	Three bears were reported on the greenway at the golf course.
Friday, August 31, 2012	A bear was reported having been frequenting a residential porch at 1 Mile Haines Highway.
Saturday, September 15, 2012	A bear was reported getting into a freezer at Chilkoot Estates. Police scared the bear off with a siren.
Tuesday, September 25, 2012	A caller reported that a bear made contact with the rear side of his truck as he was turning onto Deishu drive; an officer responded but did not make contact with the bear.
Friday, March 15, 2013	1535: Dispatch received a call to report a bear has returned to the dump and was damaging the building. AST advised.
Friday, May 24, 2013	1828: Caller reported that he had been followed by a brown bear (no cubs visible) for about 1.5 miles on Lutak Road while he was riding his bicycle.
Friday, June 14, 2013	2000: An individual called to report that a bear had charged and swiped at their vehicle Lutak Road. The park ranger and officers were advised. Officers were unable to locate the bear.

Friday,
September 6,
2013

Multiple callers reported a brown bear cub near the harbor. They were advised to call back if the bear became a threat to life or property.

Friday, September 6, 2013	1900: A caller reported someone firing firecrackers at the bear on the beach. Police reported that they were firing "flash-bangs" to move the bear into the woods.
Friday, November 1, 2013	2208: A caller reported seeing a bear leaning on a glass window of a residence on Mud Bay Road. The bear left when the resident tapped on the window. Wildlife authorities were advised.
Monday, June 16, 2014	0053: A caller from the Fort Seward area reported hearing sounds of a bear in the vicinity. He was advised that the occurrence of bears in the area at this time of year is inevitable. The caller reported no actual sighting of an actual bear. Police were advised.
Friday, June 27, 2014	1133: A pedestrian male at 5 Mile Lutak contacted police to advise of bears in the area and in the bushes. Police responded after being advised that the caller's concern was the bears possibly going into traffic. The caller was advised that bears in that area are common at this time of year. Police made contact with the male who stated he was fine and had a whistle and would contact police if he needed assistance.
Thursday, July 31, 2014	0131: A caller on Front Street reported seeing headlights pointing into her residence off of Lutak and was concerned that perhaps the car was the police spotting a bear in the area. She was advised to proceed as if there were a bear and not venture outside. Car lights were not from the police.
Wednesday, August 14, 2014	1710: A bear sow was reported as charging at a man working at the dump. The bear had reportedly already had a cub killed by another bear earlier in the last few days. The man was unhurt and retreated to the office.

Wednesday, August 14, 2014	1855: A caller reported a bear cub apparently looking for its mother on Fair Drive. The caller advised that she gave a child out walking a ride through the area so as to avoid the bear.
Sunday, August 17, 2014	1811: Small Tracts resident reporting sow with two cubs attempted to enter the residence. Caller reported the mother had placed paws on door and pushed. Officer responded to area, unable to locate sow.
Sunday, August 17, 2014	1813: Bear Trail Lane residence reporting two cubs on their porch possibly attempting to enter the house. Officer responded but the sow and two cubs had left the area.
Thursday, August 28, 2014	0030: A caller reported a sow and two cubs attempting to gain access into a garbage shed on Beach Road. HBPD advised.
Thursday, August 28, 2014	0600: A caller reported scaring off two large brown bears at the Chilkoot Indian Association (CIA) Subdivison. HBPD advised.
Thursday, August 28, 2014	0730: A caller on Cathedral View reported a bear had gotten into their storage shed in the night. Wildlife troopers were advised.
Thursday, August 28, 2014	0930: A caller at Community Waste Solutions called to report a sow and two cubs at the facility. The complainant called back to report that a citizen had come and helped scare the bear away. The complainant called back a third time to report that the bears were back. A HBPD officer responded and assisted in scaring off the bears. AST also notified.
Saturday, August 30, 2014	Caller reported people getting too close to bears at the fish weir on the Chilkoot River. AST advised.

Saturday, August 30, 2014	2138: A caller reported returning bears, a sow and cub, on Sunshine. She stated the bears had gotten into garbage and dog food the day before and now those items had been removed but the bears had come back. She was only wishing to report the incident. HBPD and F&G advised.
Sunday, August 31, 2014	1238: A caller living on Cathedral View reported a bear got in his truck bed and took a cooler of fresh fillets from the under the canopy. AST advised. Another caller also reported a bear in the same area.
Monday, September 1, 2014	2030: A caller on Beach Road reported that there were two bears getting into a garbage dumpster. A HBPD officer responded and scared away the bear.
Wednesday, September 3, 2014	0030: A caller in the Fort Seward area called to report that it sounded like a bear was currently getting into something at Mosey's Cantina Restaurant. Bears had gotten into the dumpster. Community Waste Solutions removed the dumpster.
Wednesday, September 3, 2014	0730: A caller reported that there was a sow and two cubs at the Community Waste Solutions landfill. HBPD officer responded and the bears were chased away into the woods above the landfill. AST and F&G notified.
Saturday, September 6, 2014	0148: A caller living on Newhart near FAA reported someone had apparently vandalized her yard by scattering trash on her lawn. Requested to speak with officers in the morning. HBPD officer responded and met with caller and investigated scene. Officers suggested a bear made the mess.

Sunday, September 7, 2014	A woman came to the station and reported a bear had tried to get into her car during the night. She did not provide a residence. Wildlife troopers were advised.
Sunday, September 7, 2014	1904: A caller on the 911 line reported seeing two bears in the Carr's Cove area, not causing damage, just walking. Dispatch told the caller to not use the emergency line to report bears that were just walking and not causing damage.
Saturday, September 27, 2014	0200: A caller living on Chilkoot Drive reported a bear tipped over a bear proof garbage can. The caller scared the bear away into the woods, but thought he could still see the bear's eyes shining. The caller was advised to stay inside and keep his dog in, too. HBPD, AST, and F&G notified.
Friday, October 3, 2014	0614: A caller in the Chilkoot Subdivison reporting more than one bear attempting to get into a bear proof trash can and pushing the can around. Police were advised. The caller was advised to remain indoors. HBPD officer advised.
Sunday, October 5, 2014	0303: A resident of Small Tracts Road called to report shooting a large female sow that had entered on to his residence porch. A shot was fired to scare the bear away, but it came back and charged at the resident who shot the bear. HBPD officer responded and met with resident. AST and F&G also contacted. Sow reported to have two large cubs with her, but the cubs had run off into the woods. F&G follow up - will try to locate cubs for transfer.
Monday, October 6, 2014	0600: Caller at 3 Mile Haines Highway called to report that a bear had gotten into their garbage container. HBPD, AST, and F&G notified.

Tuesday, October 7, 2014	0300: Caller on Small Tracts Road reported a bear had broken into their truck. The caller did not know at the time if the truck had sustained damages. Caller advised he would call back if damaged - no call back received. HBPD, AST, and F&G advised.
Wednesday, October 8, 2014	0543: Caller living in the Chilkoot Subdivison reported a bear had tipped over the dumpster. A HBPD officer responded and scared off the bear, which was carrying away a garbage bag from the dumpster.
Thursday, October 9, 2014	Caller reported a very large bear had broken into a metal shed on Highland and taken a trash bag away. A HBPD officer responded, but the bear had left the premises. AST and F&G notified.
Saturday, October 11, 2014	0240: A resident living on Barnett Drive called to report that he had fired one shot to scare off a bear. The bear ran away and is no longer in the area. HBPD, AST, and F&G notified.
Saturday, October 11, 2014	0736: Another resident on Barnett Drive called to report that sometime during the night a bear had torn his garage door open and scattered trash. The caller advised the bear was no longer in the area. HBPD, AST, and F&G notified.
Sunday, October 12, 2014	0019: A resident of the Chilkoot Subdivison called to advise the bears were trying to get into the dumpsters again. The caller requested HBPD come out and shoot the bears, as he is tired of them, and he has to walk in that area regularly. HBPD, AST, and F&G notified.
Sunday, October 12, 2014	A Dusty Trails resident reported two bears had gotten into the trash at the apartments and left with a trash bag. Police, troopers and F&G were advised.

Monday, October 13, 2014	1930: A Haines School official reported being stuck in the school due to a dumpster diving bear in the school lot. A HBPD officer responded and scared the bear off. AST and F&G notified.
Tuesday, October 14, 2014	1700: The Haines High School requested a patrol drive by due to recent bear activity. There was a late activity finishing up at the school. A HBPD officer was advised and responded to the school and stood by until the Haines Glacier Bears were gone - no other real bears in the area *(Editor's note: the athletic teams of the Haines High School are named the "Haines Glacier Bears").*
Saturday, October 25, 2014	2135: A school employee called requesting police to drive through the school lot near the gym as there were two large brown bears trying to tip over the dumpster. Police responded and found the dumpsters turned over and bears gone. The school dance continued without further incident. AST and F&G notified.
Sunday, November 16, 2014	0255: A resident living on Deishu Drive called to report hearing what she thought might be a bear on her porch. She was asked to look out the window to see if there was a bear, and she reported there was a man. A HBPD officer responded to the residence, and discovered the man was the caller's boyfriend. He had been asked to leave, but had stayed on the porch. He left.

MOOSE	
Saturday, January 16, 2010	Caller reported a moose stuck in the river at 29.5 Mile Haines Highway. AST advised.
Wednesday, March 31, 2010	Caller reported they hit a moose at 10 Mile Haines Highway, no one in the vehicle was injured and the moose ran off. AST and officer advised.
Friday, April 9, 2010	Multiple people reported a moose calf was hit by a vehicle at 3 Mile Haines Highway. An officer responded.
Saturday, April 10, 2010	Caller would like to be on the list for the moose meat.
Sunday, April 11, 2010	Caller complained about a gut pile left on their private property after people collected the moose meat from a road kill.
Friday, May 7, 2010	Caller reported broken mirror debris on Haines Highway from a moose kill. Officer advised.
Monday, June 28, 2010	Caller reported eagles swooping down on something in the Chilkat River at 6.5 Mile Haines Highway. Troopers found a dead moose.
Wednesday, September 8, 2010	Troopers were advised that a moose was floating down the river at 19 Mile Haines Highway.
Friday, September 17, 2010	An officer responded to a call complaining that moose hunters were pointing guns toward the Haines Highway at the airport. The officer found no one.

Wednesday, October 13, 2010	Caller reported a moose hit and killed by a vehicle at 5 Mile Haines Highway. The vehicle was gone when police and troopers arrived. The meat was donated to charity.
Tuesday, February 22, 2011	Caller reported an aggressive female moose with calf on Mosquito Lake Road. AST advised.
Friday, March 4, 2011	Caller reported a moose hit by a truck on the Haines Highway. Officer responded and disposed of the badly injured moose.
Thursday, March 17, 2011	Caller reported that they were told about a moose that charged and struck a pedestrian on Mud Bay Road. Officer advised.
Thursday, May 19, 2011	Caller reported a cow moose with two newborn calves in front of the school that is causing concern for people trying to enter and exit the school. Officer responded and provided security until everybody had left the school. The moose bedded down in the grassy area next to the gym and would not cause any disruption for the night.
Friday, May 20, 2011	Person reported the mother moose and calves are still at the school and classes would be starting soon. Police, Alaska State Troopers and Borough Public Works responded and moved the moose off to a safer spot until the newborn calves will be strong enough to go outside of town.
Wednesday, May 25, 2011	Person came to the window at the police station and stated that their dog had just been attacked by the moose that is living in the woods right across the street from the police station. The dog had only been hit once by the moose in the hip. The dog was not bleeding or limping. Officer advised.

Monday, May 30, 2011	Caller reported a mother moose with two calves walking down by the harbor and there were some people trying to walk towards her. Officer responded and the moose went into a wooded area.
Sunday, June 5, 2011	Caller reported a moose in town near the library. An officer advised the caller not to approach the moose.
Thursday, June 16, 2011	Caller reported hitting a moose at the 14-15 Mile straight stretch. AST advised and charity called to respond and dispose of the moose.
Monday, October 3, 2011	Caller reporting a moose had been hit at 27 Mile Haines Highway. AST advised and a charity was contacted to dispose of the moose.
Saturday, January 21, 2012	Caller reported a moose and calf were seen going into a parking lot near 3rd Avenue where the snowplows push the snow.
Monday, January 30, 2012	A dead moose was reported at 17 Mile Haines Highway after being hit by a vehicle. AST was advised and the moose was salvaged for charity.
Thursday, February 16, 2012	A moose at 11 Mile Haines Highway was hit by a vehicle and killed. A charity was called to salvage the meat.
Friday, March 30, 2012	Caller reported that two moose attacked and injured a woman at 3 Mile Haines Highway. The woman received minor injuries when she fell to the ground to avoid a moose.
Friday, April 13, 2012	Caller reported hitting a moose at 5 Mile Haines Highway. The moose appeared to be fine, the vehicle sustained damage. AST was notified.
Wednesday, May 16, 2012	Caller reported a moose wandering in a residential neighborhood.

Wednesday, May 16, 2012	A caller complained over concern for a baby moose who was separated from its mother across the river. An officer responded. Later the baby and mother were bedded down together. AST advised.
Thursday, June 14, 2012	A Young Road resident reported a moose with two calves in their yard eating the landscape. Officer responded and observed the moose moving to a different location.
Thursday, June 28, 2012	There were several reports of a mother moose and 3 calves roaming the downtown area.
Thursday, December 20, 2012	A dead moose was reported at 24 Mile Haines Highway, apparently killed by a vehicle. AST advised and charity removed the moose.
Monday, April 1, 2013	0801: A wildlife call was received by dispatch reporting two very large moose walking on Haines Highway between Fair Drive and Haines Borough School System. An officer responded and followed the moose tracks which lead off into the trees but was unable to locate the moose.
Wednesday, May 29, 2013	Caller reported a moose calf on the edge of the Chilkat River in the Eagle Preserve. Wildlife troopers were already aware of the situation and letting nature take its course.
Tuesday, June 11, 2013	2308: Caller reported a moose and a calf in the road. An officer responded and determined that the moose had moved off the road and was not a traffic hazard.
Friday, September 21, 2013	A bull moose was reported ramming the fence at the Tank Farm and causing a traffic jam on Lutak Road. By the time police arrived the moose had left the scene.

Wednesday, December 18, 2013	2107: A moose was reported as having been hit by a vehicle at about 16 Mile Haines Highway. The vehicle operator dialed 911 shortly thereafter to report having hit the moose. Charity organizations were notified to harvest the moose.
Wednesday, June 11, 2014	Caller on Mud Bay Road reported he had shot a moose which had charged him twice. Wildlife troopers responded and investigated. The Haines Volunteer Fire Department received the salvaged meat.
Saturday, September 27, 2014	1841: A caller requested assistance with a moose kill. They were put in contact with the wildlife trooper.

EAGLES	
Monday, February 22, 2010	Caller reported an injured eagle was being taken to the Bald Eagle Foundation and needed medical supplies from HARK. HARK advised.
Wednesday, April 21, 2010	Caller reported two eagles tangled up together on Letnikof. AST responded.
Sunday, April 10, 2011	A person reported an eagle swimming in the bay. The American Bald Eagle Foundation was advised.

Sunday, April 10, 2011	Caller reported an eagle caught in wire with two broken legs. The Bald Eagle Foundation was advised, captured the eagle, and sent it to the Juneau Raptor Center.
Tuesday, August 16, 2011	Caller reported a dead eagle on a Mud Bay beach. The American Bald Eagle Foundation said the eagle died of natural causes.
Sunday, August 21, 2011	Caller said an eaglet had fallen from its nest. The American Bald Eagle Foundation was advised and found the eaglet could fly and still was being fed by other eagles.
Friday, June 29, 2012	A caller reported an injured eagle near Cemetery Hill; American Bald Eagle Foundation notified. Caller later reported that the eagle had moved on and was possibly not injured; Bald Eagle Foundation updated.
Wednesday, July 17, 2013	Caller reported seeing an eagle swimming in Letnikof Cove that was unable to fly once on land. The Eagle Foundation was contacted and advised eagles need an hour to dry off before flying. The caller reported the eagle had flown away.

32

HORSES	
Saturday, April 17, 2010	A person reported two horses loose near the softball fields. Officers and trooper responded.
Tuesday, March 15, 2011	Caller reported horses loose on Small Tracts Road. Officer advised. The owners eventually caught the horses.
Friday, March 18, 2011	Caller reported a pony running loose on Haines Highway. The owner was contacted and caught the pony, taking it home.
Saturday, May 7, 2011	Caller reported *a horse tied to a pickup truck in front of a local bar.* Caller was concerned the horse might get hit as it was in the lane of traffic. Officer responded and made contact with the owner. Officer also concluded there was no current traffic hazard.
Tuesday, June 14, 2011	Officer helped corral a loose horse.
Wednesday, June 15, 2011	Caller reported two horses loose on Mud Bay Road. Officer advised.
Sunday, June 19, 2011	Caller reported horses loose on Letnikof. Horse owner advised.
Tuesday, July 12, 2011	Caller reported a horse loose on Small Tracts Road. An officer responded and returned the horse to its home.
Sunday, September 4, 2011	Caller reported a brown and white horse running loose on Small Tracts Road. Officer responded.
Monday, September 12, 2011	Caller reported two horses running loose on Small Tracts Road. Owner advised.
Tuesday, January 10, 2012	Caller reported a horse near a business on Main Street. The owner was advised and went to secure the horse.

Thursday, January 12, 2012	Caller reported a loose horse on Small Tracts Road due to a broken fence. The owner was contacted and the horse was secured.
Tuesday January 17, 2012	Caller reported a loose horse on the Haines Highway. The owner was notified to secure her horse.
Friday, February 2, 2013	Caller reported a horse loose in the Sawmill Road area. Police responded but the horse had already been contained.
Sunday, March 31, 2013	Dispatch received a report of a horse loose at 3 Mile Haines Highway. An officer was able to put the horse back in its pen and a message was left for the owner.
Sunday, April 21, 2013	Police assisted with returning a horse to its paddock on Haines Highway.
Sunday, May 5, 2013	There was a report of a horse that was on the Haines Highway that almost got struck by a vehicle. The officer responded and the owner was advised.
Thursday, May 9, 2013	Caller reported a horse in the roadway at 3 Mile Haines Highway. Police responded and found the horse had been placed back in its stall by the responsible party.
Friday, June 7, 2013	1938: A horse was reported in the area of Small Tracts Road. Officers responded and the horse was taken back to the owners.
Wednesday, July 17, 2013	1337: A horse was reported loose on Haines Highway. The owner was contacted and advised she would find someone to put the horse back in the stable.
Monday, June 2, 2014	A horse was reported to be loose *at the airport*. Police responded and found that the horse had been secured at its residence by the owner.

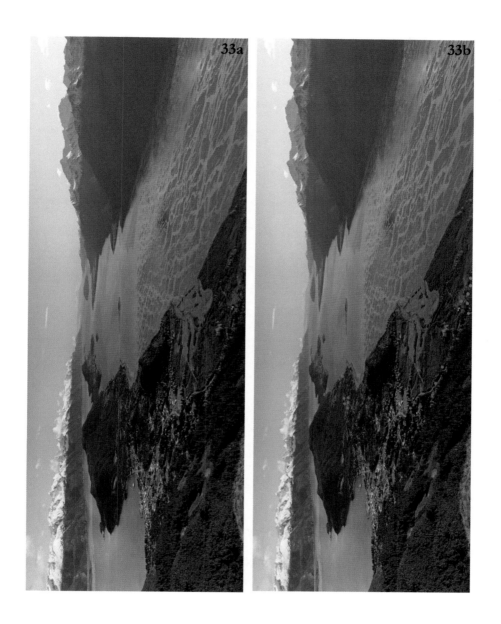

Map (approximate) of wayward horses.
Photo available at ronphotos@hotmail.com

DOGS	
Wednesday, June 23, 2010	An officer shot a Taser at a dog that charged him at Deishu after three other people reported the dog charging or trying to bite them. The dog's owner was cited for allowing the dog to run.
Saturday, August 14, 2010	An officer responded to a call about a dispute between two men at the Small Boat Harbor about an unleashed dog.
Sunday, August 15, 2010	Caller reported their dog-sitter wouldn't return a dog leash. The dog-sitter told police they didn't have the leash.
Tuesday, September 7, 2010	Caller reported rude joggers who refused a request that they keep a distance from the caller's dog.
Sunday, October 24, 2010	An officer responded to a call that a neighbor's dog had been howling in its house and the owner wouldn't answer the door when they knocked.
Monday, December 20, 2010	Caller reported a person was threatening to shoot their dog. AST advised.
Thursday, January 27, 2011	Caller reported a dog being shot in Klukwan. While running loose on another person's property the dog had been shot with an air gun. The dog did not appear to be injured. AST advised.
Saturday, May 21, 2011	Caller reported a dog was locked in a car at a downtown parking lot and had been barking for two hours. Officer responded and made contact with the owner, who will move the vehicle.
Friday, May 27, 2011	The Haines Animal Rescue Kennel reported that during the night someone had broken into their facility and took two dogs. Officer responded and case initiated.

Saturday, June 18, 2011	Caller requesting police help getting their dog that was taken away several years ago in Juneau and adopted out. Officer spoke to the man and informed him there is nothing we can do for him at this time.
Sunday, June 19, 2011	Multiple callers reported a male yelling very loud in the Comstock area. Officers responded to find the man was yelling at his dog.
Thursday, August 11, 2011	Caller reported dog walkers not picking up after their dogs.
Thursday, February 9, 2012	Caller reported their dog was shot with a BB gun and their apartment broken into. Officer responded and found no signs of entry and the dog was fine.
Wednesday, February 15, 2012	A caller reported they located a BB in their dog's ear and it was removed.
Thursday, February 23, 2012	Caller reported a dog attempting to break her yard fence to make contact with her dog.
Friday, April 27, 2012	The SEARHC clinic called to report dog bite injuries to an elderly patient who had been bitten by their family dog.
Monday, July 16, 2012	A dog was reported at large at the harbor. An officer responded and found the dog tied up.
Friday, October 12, 2012	A male reported being threatened verbally and with a semi-automatic handgun over a dog encounter with a neighbor on Main Street. The male was contacted by police and advised to enter his apartment and wait. The suspect was apprehended and taken to jail.

Tuesday, June 4, 2013	A resident reported that his dog has been missing in the Mud Bay Road area and he thought he observed the dog riding in another person's vehicle. The caller was referred to HARK.
Sunday, June 9, 2013	Officers assisted troopers by responding to an assault between two females at 26 Mile Haines Highway. The dispute was over the ownership of dogs.
Friday, September 13, 2013	A guest at a Fort Seward bed and breakfast called to report a dog had swallowed raisins. The guest requested the phone number of the lodge owners so they could be notified.
Monday, November 4, 2013	A caller reported being threatened by a male neighbor during an altercation concerning where a dog relieved itself. Police responded and separated the men.
Thursday, May 8, 2014	2000: A caller reported that his dog had broken its chain and was loose in the area of 1 Mile Haines Highway.

34

	OTHER ANIMALS OF INTEREST
Tuesday, June 15, 2010	A caller reported llamas loose on Small Tracts Road.
Wednesday, June 16, 2010	A caller in a downtown apartment reported a crying cat had kept them awake all night.
Sunday, September 19, 2010	The Bald Eagle Foundation was advised after a person reported an injured crow near the bank.
Monday, September 20, 2010	A trooper requested a charity be contacted to receive a de-boned goat.
Sunday, February 6, 2011	AST & officer responded and dispatched a goat that had been hit at 7.5 Mile Haines Highway.

Wednesday, March 2, 2011	A caller reported things being thrown around on their back porch during the night at 3 Mile Haines Highway. An officer responded and thought birds had caused the noise.
Monday, March 7, 2011	A caller reported a dumpster lid open and birds scattering the garbage at a downtown business.
Wednesday, March 9, 2011	State troopers were advised of a dead fox at the cemetery.
Monday, March 14, 2011	Caller reported a local family is keeping a lynx kitten and two wolf hybrids in their backyard. AST advised.
Friday, May 13, 2011	A caller reported a rabbit that appeared to be tame on FAA Road. HARK advised.
Wednesday, May 18, 2011	A caller reported someone was threatening to kill rabbits in the Deishu area. The caller said they already had talked to HARK.
Wednesday, August 3, 2011	A caller reported a bear was at their Menaker Road property at the same time that their goat became loose, but didn't think the bear got the goat.
Friday, August 19, 2011	A caller said a crow had a broken left wing from a cat attack. The American Bald Eagle Foundation sent the crow to the Juneau Raptor Center.
Tuesday, August 23, 2011	A caller reported their goat ran away from a Menaker Road residence.
Monday, March 26, 2012	An officer requested a case number assigned for an incident the previous day involving a dog killing two rabbits in a cage on 4th Avenue.

Friday, March 30, 2012	A caller reported a large flock of ravens and crows and his concern that a downtown business was feeding them.
Sunday, May 13, 2012	A person reported a caribou hide on the beach at Mud Bay and was concerned it would be a bear attractant. Officer responded and determined the hide did not pose a problem.
Saturday, June 2, 2012	A caller requested assistance locating a pet turtle that had escaped into her yard. The caller inquired about canine search and rescue unit availability. HARK advised.
Wednesday, July 18, 2012	A subsistence fisherman near the Lutak boat ramp reported catching a whale in his net. The whale eventually freed himself from the net and the caller was able to retrieve his net. F&G advised.
Wednesday, January 30, 2013	Caller reported a coyote dragged off his dog. and later returned to his residence. The owner recovered his dog, which was later transported to the vet in Juneau. Police and troopers responded.
Monday, February 25, 2013	1900: A female reported on 911 that her dogs were unsettled, and she was concerned about wolves that had been reported as being in the area. Officers were advised and responded to check the area for wolves.
Saturday, March 16, 2013	0936: Dispatch received a call that reported two black goats on the roadway on Small Tracts Road. The owners weren't available and an officer responded and herded the goats to a wooded area.
Friday, May 10, 2013	1500: Caller in the vicinity of Kochu Island requested assistance in contacting F&G regarding an injured sea lion. She was provided with the correct number.

Monday, June 3, 2013	A caller reported a possible abandoned baby whale near Lutak Inlet. The caller said there were no other whales around it and it "appeared lost." Officers responded but could find no sign of the whale. Dispatch also tried to call the National Maine Fishery's to advise them of the situation.
Monday, June 17, 2013	A caller reported an alpaca is at the edge of the driveway at a residence on Small Tracts Road. The owner was advised and secured the animal.
Wednesday, July 17, 2013	1238: A male was reportedly taking photos of a whale that was trapped in his fishing net. Troopers, National Oceanic and Atmospheric Administration (NOAA) and the Coast Guard were advised and were en route to investigate. Local responders reported the whale had been freed and appeared to be unharmed, although some net material was still present on the whale.
Monday, August 26, 2013	A man reported he will be studying bats in Haines and wished to alert police of his activities due to the unusual nature of them.
Thursday, November 7, 2013	2157: A caller reported their pet turtle missing and requested police assistance to find it. The caller called back to report the turtle had been found by the sound of its scratching against the wall.
Monday, January 6, 2014	1227: A caller requested assistance from HARK to extricate a cat from an engine. The animal control officer called to advise the cat was out of the engine and safe.
Monday, May 26, 2014	A caller at the Small Boat Harbor reported crows and ravens in the trash.

Monday, May 26, 2014	0943: A caller in the Haines area requested assistance in getting their pet macaw out of a tree. Hark was dispatched to assist them. Caller did not provide address - HARK provided with phone number to call.
Monday, May 26, 2014	1322: A caller on Haines Highway near 2nd Avenue reported a raven had flown into a wall in their apartment building and was injured. Personnel from the American Bald Eagle Foundation were dispatched.
Saturday, June 7, 2014	0617: A caller near 3.5 Mile Haines Highway called police to report the presence of many coyotes in the area. The caller expressed concern that her dog's safety may be at risk. The call was referred to F&G and the caller was advised to restrain her dog to protect it from wildlife.
Saturday, September 6, 2014	1852: A woman came to the station requesting assistance with determining if the voltage on her electric fence was correct or harmful (she did not provide residence information). She was provided contact information for F&G and the AST Wildlife officer. She later called back, advising that she had received the answer from another person, but would call F&G and AST as well.
Sunday, September 7, 2014	1149: The woman with questions about the electric fence came back to the HBPD and reported a bear had tried to get into her car during the night (she did not provide residence information). AST Wildlife trooper responded to HBPD and met with the woman.

10) BIZARRE INCIDENTS

Thursday, March 4, 2010	A local business reported receiving a bad check from a customer. Officer responded.
Friday, March 5, 2010	A local business reported a customer who used a bad check the day before was back in their store. Officer responded and arrested the person for a felony warrant.
Monday, March 29, 2010	Caller reported a male choking a female at a local store. Officer responded and arrested the male.
Tuesday, March 30, 2010	Caller reported being hit in the head by a female. Officer responded and arrested the female.
Saturday, August 14, 2010	A borough worker responded to a call that a manhole was open at 2nd Avenue and Main Street.
Saturday, August 14, 2010	Caller said the manhole cover was off again.
Sunday, August 15, 2010	Caller reported their child had broken into their house.
Thursday, September 2, 2010	Public works was advised of an uncovered manhole on 2nd Avenue.
Sunday, November 14, 2010	Caller reported numerous vehicles were dumped on their property on Mosquito Lake Road while they were gone for a few years. Referred to troopers.
Thursday, December 30, 2010	Caller reported their VHS tape got stuck in their VCR and they were afraid it would start a fire. Caller was advised to unplug the VCR.
Saturday, January 1, 2011	Caller requested information about crossing the border from Canada to America with a U.S. warrant. Officer advised. The officer told the caller that an arrest would be made upon crossing into the United States.

Saturday, January 1, 2011	Border officers detained a person crossing the border who had a warrant for their arrest in Alaska. Officer responded and arrested the individual.
Sunday, February 13, 2011	Caller reported concern about a person living in their vehicle. Officer responded. The person had been staying in the area because it was an internet hotspot downtown.
Sunday, March 6, 2011	Caller reported he saw a bumper lying on the ground near Delta Western. Officer advised.
Thursday, March 10, 2011	Person reported a person sleeping in the Post Office. Officer responded.
Monday, March 14, 2011	Caller reported after taking a car for a test drive and putting down a $600.00 deposit, when the vehicle was returned they only received $555.00 back. Police advised caller that this was a civil matter and that the courthouse is the proper place to file a complaint.
Wednesday, March 16, 2011	Explosive found and reported at the beach on Beach Road. There will be someone guarding it until morning. Officer advised.
Saturday, April 23, 2011	Caller reported hearing a loud boom and then sporadic power at their business. Alaska Power and Telephone was advised. It was later determined a squirrel on the wire caused the electrical problems.
Tuesday, May 5, 2011	Caller reported a speeding vehicle on Mount Riley Road. The caller stated when he tried to make contact with the driver, he was flipped off. An officer responded and gave the driver a warning.

Thursday, May 7, 2011	Person came to the police station requesting medical assistance, claiming he ate a psychedelic mushroom. EMS responded and the person was taken to SEARHC clinic and treated. Officers responded as well and case was initiated.
Friday, May 27, 2011	Caller reported a vehicle parked outside of the caller's apartment and she would like it moved as she cannot walk around her apartment without it seeing her. Officer responded.
Monday, May 30, 2011	Caller reported the foam around their neighbor's hot tub caught fire. While on the phone with the caller the neighbor reported that the fire was under control. Officer responded.
Friday, June 17, 2011	Caller reported a black truck had been parked outside her apartment for 20 minutes. Caller stated the vehicle is gone now and she will shut her blinds.
Saturday, June 25, 2011	Caller reported a possible illegal tour. Officer responded but the tour provider had left before officers arrived. Two days later the tour provider was cited for providing a tour without a permit and operating a commercial passenger vehicle without a permit.
Monday, June 27, 2011	Caller reported children destroyed the ash tray at the new Port Chilkoot Dock and are now having a sword fight with traffic cones. Officer responded.
Wednesday, June 29, 2011	Caller reported someone might be taking tires off a vehicle in between the Post Office and Quick Shop. Officer responded and found a person working on their car.
Friday, July 1, 2011	Caller reported a dispute between two different barbecue parties at an RV park. Officer responded and the situation ended in a peaceful agreement.

Thursday, August 18, 2011	Caller said someone locked them in their downtown trailer and shook it, causing items to fall and break. Police said the incident likely was a prank, but are investigating.
Sunday, September 4, 2011	Caller reported a possible fire across the canal. An officer responded and declared it a navigational beacon.
Saturday, September 17, 2011	Caller reported suspicious activity on the side of the road heading out to Lutak. Officers responded and confirmed it was people working on "Clean up Haines Weekend."
Sunday, October 2, 2011	Caller reporting a vehicle in the river at 6 Mile Haines Highway. AST advised the vehicle had been there since August.
Tuesday, February 14, 2012	A suspicious vehicle parked with someone sitting inside it was reported off Main Street. An officer contacted the occupant, who was working on a computer.
Saturday, February 25, 2012	Responding to a report of an individual riding on top of a van on Front Street, an officer conducted a traffic stop and issued a citation for reckless driving. The person aloft was a visitor with a video camera.
Friday, March 2, 2012	A dispatcher from Palm Beach, Florida reported a 911 call from a person claiming to be at Porcupine Creek. The information was passed to AST, who reported that contact was made with the individual who was located in Palm Beach, Florida and was confused and had just finished watching "Gold Rush."

Saturday, March 3, 2012	An officer called from the Juneau Police Department reporting that a person in their area received a disturbing text message from a person in the Haines area. This was investigated and determined to be a message regarding a video game that was sent to a wrong number.
Thursday, May 17, 2012	A subject arrested for DWI after a traffic stop was transported to the police department and later released on their own recognizance (observed driving slowly, crossing the center line, not stopping at a stop sign, making a wide turn and not using a turn signal in the downtown area).
Friday, July 6, 2012	Caller reported a small, live-animal trap had been lost at the Parade grounds.
Friday, December 14, 2012	A 911 call was received requesting an ambulance for a male in the Mosquito Lake area who had gotten stuck in a dump truck and had been hanging upside down for several hours possibly sustaining hypothermia and an ankle injury. Ambulance responded.
Friday, January 11, 2013	Police assisted state troopers in an attempt to serve a warrant on a male cited for failure to appear on charges of assault. They checked three addresses but were unable to locate the man. Troopers later encountered the man at a business near 0 Mile Haines Highway and arrested him. The man was released on bail.
Tuesday, April 16, 2013	A caller reported that he had used a credit card for a room at a local lodging facility and chose to leave early as the room had not been cleaned. He advised that he was reporting the incident to protect himself and his credit card.

Tuesday, April 23, 2013	Police in Juneau inquired about conditions of release for a Haines man who had been apprehended in Juneau at a bar fight.
Saturday, May 11, 2013	1400: Caller requested assistance contacting the appropriate people to assist with "sealing" a bear skin. Wildlife trooper was put in contact with the caller.
Tuesday, May 14, 2013	1245: A local lodging reported that a queen sized bed had been stolen from a room. Police initiated a case on the incident. Police suspect the person who stole the bed has also been using a master key to access and use the Jacuzzi suite. Police are following several leads.
Friday, May 31, 2013	Police assisted the Juneau Police Department in serving papers on a woman getting off the ferry in Haines.
Wednesday, July 10, 2013	An anonymous caller reported an altercation outside a downtown bar resulting in two people needing an ambulance. A man had been punching a relative in the face, and multiple bar patrons attacked the man after observing the assault. The man was medevacked to Juneau.
Sunday, September 15, 2013	0416: A caller reported partiers "yelling at the moon" nearby. Police responded and the noise makers promised to quiet down.
Saturday, May 24, 2014	A Piedad resident stated they had a large box with a stuffed penguin inside stolen the prior night. Officer advised. The stuffed penguin was discovered perched on a parked pickup truck downtown and claimed by the owner.

Tuesday, June 3, 2014	0112: A caller reported a dog barking consistently all night, every night on FAA Road and that he had called numerous times. Owner of the dog was contacted and stated that there were other dogs that barked and that police could arrest the dog if they chose to. Police responded to the address but the dog was no longer outside.
Saturday, June 7, 2014	2124: Caller reported that a cruise ship in Lynn Canal did not have appropriate running lights in a low visibility situation. Officers on patrol observed a cruise ship that appeared to be sufficiently illuminated. The caller was provided with contact information for the U.S. Coast Guard.
Saturday, June 21, 2014	1108: A caller reported the theft of his penguin, again, from the tree outside his residence on Piedad Road. Police interviewed the complainant.
Wednesday, June 25, 2014	1017: A caller reported that while urinating out in the open on private property an individual was video-taping him and he felt violated. He was advised that his actions could be construed as indecent exposure if he was in fact urinating in public.
Wednesday, July 2, 2014	Caller reported that the respondent to a protective order drove by and "flipped him off" on Mud Bay Road. Police said this wasn't a violation of the protective order.
Saturday, July 5, 2014	A person came to the Police Department to report an overturned baby stroller near the Portage Cove campground. An officer investigated and found it was an abandoned old stroller used for dolls.
Friday, August 1, 2014	Caller reported a refrigerator had been left on the side of the road near the entrance to Deishu Drive with a "free" sign attached. She was concerned that a child might get inside or be hurt. Police investigated and said there were no children inside the refrigerator.

KHNS News
Yesterday

36

The Haines Borough Assembly decided Wednesday night during a special meeting not to hire   for police chief. The assembly had approved his hire   but negotiations over salary broke down late last week and   took the borough government to task for what he said was mis-representing the salary range. In email to borough officials, he called the assembly "crooks and thieves", "narrow-mined, corrupt politicians" and asked if any of them used to work in a used car lot. The assembly authorized the interim manager to continue her search for a new chief. We'll have more on this story on our Thursday evening news cast.

Thursday, August 7, 2014	2158: A caller reported hearing gun shots in the Fort Seward area. Police responded and found it to be a man cracking a whip. The male stated that he would cease the activity.
Sunday, August 10, 2014	0830: A call came in on the 911 line; the caller was attempting to confirm his reservation with Alaska SeaPlanes. The caller stated that he did not need medical assistance and he was advised to not call 911 to check on his flight.
Saturday, August 16, 2014	A Deishu Drive resident reported a missing chainsaw. Caller later reported the chain saw was found under a pile of toys in yard.
Sunday, August 17, 2014	A Comstock Road resident stated someone had entered their yard at some point the previous night, unhooked the barbecue and left their bicycle. Officers were advised.

Friday, September 5, 2014	2159: A caller on 911 requested to speak with an officer at a local hotel on 2nd Avenue. A HBPD officer met with and interviewed the caller regarding a blackout period the caller had while he was intoxicated. It was determined no crime had occurred, just severe intoxication. This was later confirmed with a meeting involving co-workers of the caller.
Monday, September 22, 2014	1800: A caller at the Small Boat Harbor stated that someone had taken a vehicle advertised as free that the caller had just gone and got the title for from the titled owner. A HBPD officer responded and met with the caller, made contact with other interested parties that had contacted the titled owner, and the whereabouts of the free vehicle is still unknown. Police said this matter wasn't a theft because the car was advertised as free. The car owner also didn't want to report the car's removal as theft.
Tuesday, September 23, 2014	Caller reported that friends of hers had vacated a rental home on Union Street. The caller reported that items that did not belong to her were placed in her vehicle by the landlord. Her vehicle was parked near the rental. An officer spoke with the caller and her friend and they advised the property was not theirs. They were advised to leave the property if it did not belong to them. They advised they were going to place it on the front porch.
Saturday, September 27, 2014	1103: A caller in the area of 4th Avenue and Union reported being harassed on Facebook. He was advised to un-friend and block the individual harassing him.
Monday, October 6, 2014	Caller reported that the free Subaru that was taken from the harbor area while the caller was getting the title from the owner, had been located and returned to him.

Wednesday, December 3, 2014	1830: A Haines resident driving on the Highway near the airport called to report seeing a green light descending from the sky and into the Takhin Valley across the river. He believed the light to be a comet. AST was advised.
Thursday, December 25, 2014 -- *this posted on the HBPD Facebook page only*	0045 - 0430: Received numerous reports of the sounds of hooves stomping on roofs, snorting of reindeer, and a fat guy in red trying to break in to homes by the chimneys. A HBPD officer drove around town like crazy trying to find this guy, but all he was able to locate was a man in a night cap (whom had drank too many night caps) standing outside in his yard looking up at the sky in amazement. With all that said and done – at least the fat guy in red didn't take any cars. Merry Christmas.

37

MY FAVORITE FACEBOOK POST OF ALL TIME:

Haines Borough Public Library
January 24

ATTENTION LIBRARY VOLUNTEERS: The volunteer refresher training originally scheduled for tomorrow at 10:30am has been RESCHEDULED for February 8 at 10:30am due to forecasted SUNNY WEATHER! Enjoy!!!

CREDITS

1. Photo of Fort Seward taken from Picture Point.
    Photographs from this book may not be copied without
    written permission. All photos taken by Dr. Selby are
    available for purchase. Contact dselby2042@gmail.com
    Dena Selby, photographer.

2. Map of Haines Townsite courtesy of the Haines Alaska
    Community Website.
    Original cartographer unknown.

3. Porcupine photograph taken at the Kroschel Films Wildlife
    Center; permission granted by Steve Kroschel.
    Dena Selby, photographer.

4. Crossing the mud flats to get to the wedding.
    Courtesy of Deborah Marshall, photographer.

5. Newspaper notice of Tim and Melina's wedding.
    Permission granted by Melina Shields.

6. A summertime windowsill on Main Street.
    Dena Selby, photographer.

7. A kiteboader near Pyramid Island representative of the area
    of the Police Blotter Report. Kiteboarder D.A. granted permission
    to reprint.
    Dena Selby, photographer.

8. A plane landing on the Highway representative of the event
    described in this Police Blotter Report.
    This photograph was actually taken in the Yukon.
    Dena Selby, photographer.

9. Rock slide at 9 Mile Haines Highway, including large boulders.
    Dena Selby, photographer.

10. Listing taken from Facebook posting on the Haines Borough
    Police Department site. Photographer of picture not identified.

11. Decoration at a summer wedding; permission granted by
     Lori Carter.
     Dena Selby, photographer.

12. E-printed by permission from Fairbanks Daily News-Miner.

13. Listing taken from Facebook posting; reprinted with permission
     from John Hagen.

14. The Haines Marching Band at the SEAK (Southeast Alaska
     State Fair Parade) the summer of 2014.
     Dena Selby, photographer.

15. Moose footprints set in the concrete at 3rd and Main Street.
     Dena Selby, photographer.

16. Totem Trot stop #12: Lookout Park Pole. A cruise ship is docked
     in the background.
     Dena Selby, photographer.

17. Autumn along the beach at Cemetery Hill, B & W.
     Dena Selby, photographer.

18. Listing taken from Facebook posting; reprinted with permission
     from John Hagen.

19. Winter on the Chilkat River facing towards Klukwan.
     Dena Selby, photographer.

20. A typical wood stove, providing heat for the winter.
     Member of Selby family, photographer.

21. Northern lights as viewed from Tanani Point.
     Dena Selby, photographer.

22. A collection of beer bottles.
     Dena Selby, photographer.

23. Listing taken from Facebook posting; reprinted with permission
     from KHNS.

24. A typical backyard burn barrel.
     Dena Selby, photographer.

25.   Brown bear sow (commonly known as "Speedy") with cub, summer 2011. The cub has a fishhook stuck in its nose, which stayed in for about two weeks.
Dena Selby, photographer.

26.   Orphan bear at the Small Boat Harbor (indicated by red arrow).
Dena Selby, photographer.

27.   Close up photograph of the orphan bear at the Small Boat Harbor.
Dena Selby, photographer.

28.   A mother sow ("Speedy") and her cub, summer 2013.
Dena Selby, photographer.

29.   Two moose in the winter snow, with an eagle viewing them from a log. Photograph taken in the Chilkat Bald Eagle Preserve.
Dena Selby, photographer.

30.   A bald eagle landing on the ice.
Dena Selby, photographer.

31.   A bald eagle swimming in the Chilkat River.
Dena Selby, photographer.

32.   Bald eagle vs. seagull stand-off over a choice piece of salmon.
Dena Selby, photographer.

33a.   The view from the top of Mount Ripinski showing the Haines penisula. Photograph by Ron Jackson; used with his permission. It may not be copied without written permission. It is available for purchase as a 12 X 31 inch panorama.
Contact ronphotos@hotmail.com
Ron Jackson, photographer.

33b.   Same photograph as 33a, overlaid with red markings showing approximate locations of wayward horses.
Ron Jackson, photographer; photo markings by Dena Selby.

34.   Red fox photo taken at the Kroschel Films Wildlife Center; permission granted by Steve Kroschel.
Dena Selby, photographer.

35. The revered raven.
     Dena Selby, photographer.

36. Listing taken from Facebook posting; reprinted with permission from KHNS.

37. Listing taken from Facebook posting on the Haines Borough Public Library site.

38. Supermoon rising across the Lynn Canal.
     Dena Selby, photographer.

39. An early morning photograph of a sow (commonly known as "White Claws") enjoying a freshly caught salmon.
     Dena Selby, photographer.

39

ABOUT THE AUTHOR

Dena Selby, M.D. is a retired Pediatric Pathologist, now devoted to her second career of photography. The Selby family has a summer house in Haines. dselby2042@gmail.com.